PRAISE FOR *DIVIDED*

The abyss between who we are and who we should be is both deep and wide. Too often we allow fear or lies to stand in the way of God's plans for our lives. In this book, Bill offers wisdom and insight that will help give you courage to walk more closely with Jesus.

—Dr. Reggie Anderson, author of *Appointments with Heaven*

Bill spoke to me in the opening sentence of this book—"I awoke in the dead of night." He goes on to describe lying awake, battling anxiety, and attempting to reconcile what he feels and what he knows to be true. Because that middle-of-the-night battle is dangerously familiar to me, I need this book. Bill, thank you for speaking with humility and wisdom to what it looks like to navigate that space between emotion and truth.

—David Thomas, therapist and author of the best-selling *Wild Things: The Art of Nurturing Boys*

One thing is sure. Bill tells the truth about himself and invites you to explore the mysterious contradiction of Jesus, "Lose your life if you wish to find it." What will you lose? Only that which keeps you divided and half alive. Don't be afraid! Bill knows the path of life and writes about it so eloquently!

—Wes Yoder, author of *Bond of Brothers: Connecting with Other Men beyond Work, Weather and Sports*

Divided is a book that has the unique ability to make the head and the heart sing together in unison, which is what God has designed for us. What makes Bill Delvaux unique is his ability to bring his years of experience as a Bible and life teacher to make this reading experience a classroom of analyzing how we leverage our passions. By reading the book, you feel that Bill is there in person, encouraging you by using great life questions and providing rich story visuals to bring you along the journey. Use caution, as this book is dangerous in that it will ignite

something inside of you to "go" and "do" what God is stirring deep inside your soul.

—Dave Schroeder, speaker and blogger at *Scenes of Life* (www .DavidMSchroeder.com)

With characteristic humility, Bill Delvaux puts a spotlight on a shared human struggle: the fear of being known. Ever since Eden we have been wearing masks and coverings to hide the things of which we are ashamed. With generous anecdotes from his own life story, Bill helps us discover the difference between a divided heart and a united heart, a discovery that can move us toward spiritual, emotional, and personal freedom. When we are at our best and when we are at our worst, Jesus assures us that we are known *and* loved, exposed *and* not rejected. When we are able to lay hold of this, we are then free to become the best expressions of our unique selves. I highly recommend this book.

—Scott Sauls, senior pastor of Christ Presbyterian Church in Nashville, TN

Bill Delvaux addresses one of the most foundational issues in life— identity. It is not too far reaching to say that many of us have no idea who we are. We know our title, our role, and the expectations others have of us, but we wander into church, the workplace, and our homes without a solid understanding of our eternal value. *Divided* reminds me that I am a treasured possession of God, and it is from that platform that all of life has its true meaning. Thank you, Bill, for reminding me of the bridge that spans all the gaps in life—God loves me and always will!

—Dr. Craig Fry, president, Christian Leadership Concepts

Bill Delvaux diagnoses our common disease with exquisite care and offers a gracious cure. This book is a must-read for any Christian longing for a more authentic, integrated life.

—Nathan E. Larkin, founder of the Samson Society and author of *Samson and the Pirate Monks: Calling Men to Authentic Brotherhood*

As part of our human condition, we have learned to stay in our heads and not connect with the realities and feelings of our hearts. Bill Delvaux has not only addressed how we have arrived at this place, but writes in a way that helps us see the problem and how we got there and then leads us back to a place of wholeness where the heart and the head are connected. *Divided* invites us to look at our own disconnection and then offers us the hope of becoming reconnected, undivided.

—Gail Worsham Pitt, director of Dovehouse Ministries

Bill Delvaux's honesty in this book is refreshing. The way he pursues truth and asks questions makes this book accessible to many. I feel like he has put words to my own journey of closing the great divide.

—Mary Beth Chapman, president of Show Hope and wife of Steven Curtis Chapman

Every day I become more aware of the need to be whole, to once and for all fill in this great divide that separates me from the freedom I so long to embrace in myself. It is a journey that must be taken if we are to ever know true joy. This book will awaken in you the desire to find that freedom once and for all.

—Scott Reall, founder and executive director of Restore Ministries and author of *Journey to Freedom*

In *Divided*, Bill invites each of us to see and voice our own stories of disintegration and respond to the Father who pursues and welcomes, heals and liberates broken people just like me. I am so grateful for my friend's life and his insight into the ways of the heart and the riches of God's grace.

—Dr. Scotty Ward Smith, author of *EveryDay Prayers: 365 Days to a Gospel-Centered Faith*; *Objects of His Affection*; *The Reign of Grace*; and *Restoring Broken Things*

DIVIDED

WHEN THE HEAD AND HEART DON'T AGREE

BILL DELVAUX

THOMAS NELSON
Since 1798

NASHVILLE   MEXICO CITY   RIO DE JANEIRO

Published in Nashville, Tennessee, by Thomas Nelson. Thomas Nelson is a registered trademark of HarperCollins Christian Publishing, Inc.

Published in association with J. David Huffman for MAE/brandWAVESLLC

Page Design and Layout: Crosslin Creative

Thomas Nelson titles may be purchased in bulk for educational, business, fund-raising, or sales promotional use. For information, please e-mail SpecialMarkets@Thomas Nelson.com.

Unless otherwise indicated, Scripture quotations are taken from The Voice™ translation. © 2012 Ecclesia Bible Society. Used by permission. All rights reserved.

Scripture quotations marked NIV are taken from the Holy Bible, New International Version®, NIV®. Copyright © 1973, 1978, 1984, 2011 by Biblica, Inc.™ Used by permission of Zondervan. All rights reserved worldwide. *www.zondervan.com.*

* Note: Italics in quotations from The Voice are used to "indicate words not directly tied to the dynamic translation of the original language" but that "bring out the nuance of the original, assist in completing ideas, and . . . provide readers with information that would have been obvious to the original audience" (The Voice, preface).

ISBN: 978-0-5291-2126-4

Printed in the United States of America

15 16 17 18 19 20 RRD 6 5 4 3 2 1

To my mother and father:
The older I get, the more thankful I am for each of you.

CONTENTS

ACKNOWLEDGMENTS

Thanks to David Huffman, my agent, for opening the door for this book when no door was even visible. You have done it again.

Thanks to Frank Couch and Maleah Bell, my editors at Thomas Nelson. Thank you for believing in me and being a joy to work with.

Thanks to Kate Armstrong for finding the way to tell the whole story of this book in one simple cover drawing.

Thanks to the class of adults at West End Community Church who listened to this material as I was writing it and offered helpful feedback.

Thanks to countless friends who read parts of the manuscript and encouraged me to keep writing.

Thanks to all the men and women who have honored me with your stories.

Thanks to the board of Landmark Journey Ministries. Your willingness to go on this crazy adventure with me continues to amaze and humble me.

Thanks to John Eldredge of Ransomed Heart and Curt Thompson of Being Known. Your thoughts are so much a part of me that they are now almost impossible to separate out.

Thanks to Leanne Payne and Sarah Young, women who know the presence of God and whose words have enlightened me in the deep places.

Thanks to all the authors from the past who are quoted in this book. Your voices continue to father and nourish me. I can't wait to meet you all one day.

Thanks to Carter, my fellow warrior, for talking me off the cliff at moments when things got tough as I was writing.

Thanks to Bruce and Matt for our continued conversations of the heart on Friday mornings.

Thank you to Rachel and Abigail. You continue to make my life as a father one of joy and hope.

Thank you to Heidi. No words could speak what I feel. Thank you for twenty-eight years together. And yes, the best is yet to come.

Thank You, Jesus. I am stunned. Your presence has changed everything for me as a man. One day it will change the whole world.

INTRODUCTION
STALKED IN THE NIGHT

*What else doth anxiety about the future
bring thee but sorrow upon sorrow?*

—Thomas à Kempis[1]

I awoke in the dead of night. Glancing at my watch, I saw the time: 4:30 a.m. *Nope, not time to get up. Perhaps I can roll over and go back to sleep.* Instead, my mind quickly veered in another direction, to a book I had tried to start writing. And with that one mental turn, anxiety began to trickle into my stomach. The book had not been going well. Starting it had felt like an old car jerking into motion and then sputtering out. I fretted over the thesis, I was confused about the chapters, and after repeated attempts, I was getting nowhere. With that realization hitting me in the dark, anxiety now began to grip me like a steel claw. *Can I pull this book off? Perhaps this is beyond me.*

Then my thoughts took another turn, to my present circumstances. They weren't good either. With the help of some friends, I had spent the last year trying to forge a new ministry to men. It had felt like trying to hack my way through tangled undergrowth. Nothing about it had been easy: structuring small groups, planning events, promoting on social media, attempting to find a niche. On top of all that was the fund-raising. I had so little previous experience, yet I had plunged into it with the necessary calls and conversations. That, too, had been difficult, harder than I could have imagined, with the undergrowth refusing me passage. And now the reality was becoming starkly clear with the bank account. We were running out of money.

So much seemed at stake now, not just the ministry, but the future—for our family, our living situation, our stability, our security. It all seemed on the line. The level of anxiety turned up another notch and rose to a screech. But now it had another companion, one that had stalked me so often in the past: fear.

Realizing I was never going back to sleep, I got up, made my morning coffee, and took it out on the back porch. As I do most early mornings, I opened my Bible, trying to hear it attentively. But this morning, all I could hear was the fear, and it was screaming at me. Reading the Scriptures felt like trying to focus on a textbook in Swahili. It was print on a page, making no impression, offering no help. Instead my thoughts kept circling back around to the book. I had gotten the green light from an editor to submit a proposal for it after a lunchtime conversation. It was a remarkable opportunity that I was not going to let slip away. At first it seemed like an exciting topic, one that was so interwoven with my story, one I had already taught to others. Here was something I could really pull off, some-thing that could help others and expand God's kingdom. But at every turn, I had met obstacles, roadblocks, detours, and then dead ends. I couldn't get it moving.

Abruptly it all came to me—why I was so fearful. No matter what I told myself, I really wasn't writing this book for others or for the Lord. I was writing it for myself, for the potential money it could offer. I had already figured out how the book advance could tide me over, stemming the hemorrhage of funds from the ministry account. But with no book coming, there would be no money. The more I tried to think my way out of the mess, the more fear rampaged through me.

Then it happened. I suddenly jolted up out of my fear and saw it. I couldn't believe I had missed it. Everything I was now wrestling with was exactly what the whole book was about. All the truths concerning God's provision, all the commands not to be fearful, things I had known and taught—it all seemed like life on an alien planet. Instead what felt painfully true was my anxiety over the book and my fear of financial ruin. And underneath all that was a tenaciously held belief: it was up to me to figure it all out. The truths of Scripture seemed locked away in some mental closet, inaccessible, with no doorknob. What I knew had nothing to do with what I felt. I was a divided man.

My thoughts now turned again, this time to a conversation with a young man on the back porch that previous evening. He had come over to process some family and job issues, but that was just the surface of things as we descended into the real mess. It concerned a young woman to whom he was attracted. As we dialogued, he admitted to a pattern with every romantic inclination. There was first an idealization, vaulting her up as something perfect, beyond compare. Then came the inevitable collapse, a realization that she wasn't perfect, and with that a compulsive annoyance with some particular fault she had. No matter how hard he tried to reason his way out of it, the same pattern always haunted him. It had ruined every relationship in the past, and it was about to ruin this one. I asked him if he had any idea what was behind this. His response was so instructive: "I can give you the Sunday school answer: I'm trying to find in a woman the satisfaction I'm supposed to find in God."

He knew the right answer, but it wasn't helping him one bit. Here was a young man whose life was exemplary in so many ways, whose faith appeared strong, and yet underneath, anxiety and obsession plagued him, especially in his dealings with women. In a pleading voice he wanted to know how to make the compulsion go away. He was stuck, fearful that this would never change. The answer he could recite had no connection to the pulls in his heart. He, too, was a divided man.

What I was wrestling with, what that young man was wrestling with, is a divide, a deep fault line that runs through the consciousness of everyone you know and everyone you will ever meet. It's a split that runs through you as well. For we are all divided beings, tossed and blown by clashing desires. It's a conflict that drives so much of our misery and confusion. Tragically for some, it's a conflict that drives them until they catapult over an edge. For others, it drives them to give up and waste away.

We accept this divided life without question as normative, that the conflicted life is the only life. But what if it's not the norm? What if it's abnormal, the corruption? What if the divide we feel is some-thing that could be closed, even if just partially in this life? What if what we knew to be true and what we experienced in life could somehow be reconciled, could somehow make more contact? What if the pages of the Bible could become more of a felt reality in our daily experience? This book is about that possibility, about the journey to close the divide—what it looks like, and what it will mean for those who choose such a path. It's a journey that will lead us into narrow places of confusion and terror, opening up into landscapes of wonder and beauty. It's a journey I have been on, along with other close companions. It's a journey I invite you on as well.

One last thing you need to know. The book that I couldn't write eventually became a reality. My divided soul closed a bit that anxious morning, and I was no longer stalked by fear. Healing came, and soon after that, the words came. So I started writing.

It's the book you now hold.

PART I

VIEWING THE DIVIDE

How It Began and What It Destroys

> They [Adam and Eve] sat them down to
>   weep; nor only tears
> Rained at their eyes, but high winds worse
>   within
> Began to rise, high passions, anger, hate,
> Mistrust, suspicion, discord, and shook sore
> Their inward state of mind, calm region once
> And full of peace, now tossed and turbulent.
>   —John Milton, *Paradise Lost*

Yet, man did not so fall away from Being as to be absolutely nothing, but in so far as he turned himself toward himself, he became less than he was when he was adhering to Him who is supreme Being. Thus, no longer to be in God but to be in oneself in the sense of to please oneself is not to be wholly nothing but to be approaching nothingness.

—Augustine[1]

We all long for Eden, and we are constantly glimpsing it: our whole nature at its best and least corrupted, its gentlest and most human, is still soaked with the sense of exile.

—J. R. R. Tolkien[2]

So the Eternal God banished Adam *and* Eve from the garden of Eden *and exiled humanity from paradise, sentencing humans to laborious lives* working the very ground man came from.

—Genesis 3:23

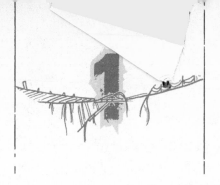

THE DIVIDE OPENS

For there are two distinct sorts of ideas:
those that proceed from the head and
those that emanate from the heart.

—**Alexandre Dumas**[1]

At twelve years old, I was a generally carefree boy. But as I entered an all-boys school in the seventh grade, insecurity began to edge in on me. I still enjoyed my studies, and the teachers all seemed to be pleased with me, but like most boys that age, I longed to be liked and affirmed by my classmates. The worst thing that could ever happen would be to do something to expose myself to scorn. I quickly learned to avoid anything that would trigger such a response. I saw what happened to boys who were mocked. It wasn't pretty. Yet, despite all of my best-laid plans, what I dreaded became reality.

It happened during the doldrums of that winter when the teacher suddenly announced that we would be having a basketball tournament between the three seventh-grade homerooms. It was supposed to be a welcome diversion to break up the grayness and chill of the season. She then read off a list of names that had been picked to represent our homeroom as a team. I snapped to attention when I heard my name called, almost in disbelief. Why would they pick me? I had never played basketball on the school's team or been coached in the sport. Sure, I had shot the ball a few times at the goal in our driveway, but beyond that, I didn't even know the rules. Being a compliant boy, however, I didn't resist or object. I just accepted it as inevitable.

I clearly remember walking to the gym feeling like a lamb going to the slaughter. I knew deep down that no matter how hard I tried, no matter how much I wanted to show everyone that I could play the game, it wasn't going to go well. I was trapped, sensing something ominous approaching, with no way to stop it. I entered the gym feeling as if thousands of eyes were watching me, assessing me, judging me. After a few opening announcements, the tournament began. The ominous was now bearing down on me. Soon into the game, the dreaded moment arrived: I got called out on the court.

I remember hustling my way up and down the gym floor, trying to mimic what other boys were doing. Yet instead of going after the ball, I was terrified of it. I didn't even know how to dribble, much less shoot accurately. To attempt either of these maneuvers would expose me to failure before the eyes of every seventh grader. I was sure the ridicule would then soon follow. So whenever the ball came to me, I would hand it off as quickly as possible to someone who seemed to know what he was doing. But even with that maneuver, I still felt useless and inept, unable to do something that seemed to be expected of every boy that age. Worst of all, I felt stripped naked in front of everyone. My secret was out. I left the game in shock, with my soul hemorrhaging and no way to stop the bleed.

For whatever reason, the sense of shame that day felt so searing, so defining, that I was never the same carefree person again. That boy died on the basketball court that day. Life now became precarious and unpredictable. Something like this could easily happen again. I became watchful, wary, self-protective. A deep shift occurred inside, locking me into a pattern, forcing me to submit to a nameless, voiceless compulsion. What I now offered to those around me was always a scripted performance. I avoided anything that smelled of risk. And the fact that the compulsion was nameless and voiceless only gave it more power. I had no idea what *it* was.

Years later, at the instigation of a friend and counselor, I pulled up the basketball story I had buried for so long, finally putting words to the event. Along with the story came something else unexpected. It was the nameless, voiceless thing, now finding its voice. This is what I heard: *I will never do anything to make me feel this way again. I will never expose myself like this. I will never, ever fail in front of others.* It was an oath to which I had pledged my heart with an obsessive devotion. This was the opening of a divide in me, a rip in the fabric of my being that would only widen and deepen in the coming years. Ironically, my attempts at protecting myself from further failure only made me more vulnerable to other unspoken vows, more voiceless commitments.

A couple of years later, the tenderness and affection of a certain girl seized me. I felt safe around her and free to fling away the masks. I was experiencing the euphoria of truly connecting to someone, of being in love for the first time. But she was dating someone else

---

A deep shift occurred inside, locking me into a pattern, forcing me to submit to a nameless, voiceless compulsion.

at the time, an accomplished athlete and the quarterback of a high school football team. Following the love I felt and continuing to pursue her now meant risking rejection by her or conflict with her boyfriend. Something inside me collapsed. I knew I could never compete with him. Besides, I was too committed to self-protection for that. So one day, without explanation, I just walked away from her, making another unspoken promise to myself: *If loving feels like this, I will never love again.* The divide had cut into me deeper.

During that same time, another event crystallized a third commitment. I had never excelled in athletics. After the basketball disaster, the possibility of failure was such a living terror that I never seriously considered most sports. But track was different. During the eighth grade, I discovered that I was fast. In fact, I became one of the fastest sprinters on the team, running the 400-meter open and the sprint relays. But as I returned to track my freshman year, I noticed that two of my former teammates were starting to keep up with me on the 400. And by my sophomore year, they began to pass me. No matter how hard I tried to stay up with them, they always managed to pull away halfway into the run. I felt deflated and ashamed. I was failing in front of others again, something intolerable to me. So during the middle of the season that year, I lied and told the coach I was tired of track and wanted to quit. Despite his protests that day, I walked away again.

I thought I would now be free of more potential failure, keeping my first vow. But I was deceived. The fear of failure only ramped up,

"If I can't be a successful athlete, I can never be a man." That one sentence drove my compulsive idealization of sports for years, long into my coaching career.

as the divide split me deeper still, for now I had swallowed a lie that would relentlessly coerce and shame me: "If I can't be a successful athlete, I can never be a man." That one sentence drove my compulsive idealization of sports for years, long into my coaching career.

A HOLY MOMENT

I have told these three stories many times to large and small audiences, for they form the foundational structures I lived out of, dividing me from my truest self, dividing me even from God Himself. But I will never forget the time I recounted these stories to a large class of adults at the church I was attending. After my time of storytelling, I asked them to put words to some of their own voiceless beliefs and commitments. I remember an awkward silence; I knew we were entering risky waters. One man finally spoke up, and it was the last thing I expected to hear: "If I speak up, I'll look like an idiot." Ironically, he was admitting the fear and hesitation that everyone was wrestling with. His bold move opened the way for others to follow.

A woman then raised her hand and admitted, "If I'm good, nothing bad will happen." Another one offered this: "No one really cares what I say anyway." Another woman submitted this response: "If I stay disconnected, then I won't have to deal with people who hurt me." A man then recounted a recent attempt to repair something that his wife needed fixing in the house. As he admitted his shame over the failure to get the job done, he spoke this one: "I'm not man enough to figure this out." One woman, who seemed so thoughtful with her children, caught me off guard when she stated, "I'm responsible for all the pain and failure in my children." Many others then began to pour out their own hidden convictions: "If God really loved me, this wouldn't be happening to me." "If I were successful, this wouldn't be happening to me." "Why try? Nothing will change anyway." "Whatever happens, it's always my fault."

As each statement came, I wrote out the growing list for everyone to see. Then, when the hands had all been called on, I stepped back, and we all looked at the list. It was a moment of quiet wonder, approaching something almost holy, as we saw our secret convictions out on public display. Something important was happening, something groundbreaking. I could sense it.

I then put up a second list, this one consisting of basic truths from the New Testament. I formatted them like the previous list, using the first-person pronoun *I*: "I can never be separated from God's love. I will never be forsaken or abandoned by God. I cannot be condemned in Christ. I have the righteousness of Jesus. I have every spiritual blessing in Christ. I am a delight to my Father in heaven. I am forgiven and washed clean." Then I simply asked the class, "What do these two lists have to do with each other?"

I will never forget the first answer given. It was one word: "Nothing."

It's important to note that my class that day consisted of believers well tutored in the Bible. Most of them had attended church for years, having heard hundreds of sermons and countless Bible lessons. Some were even church leaders and could give good answers to theological questions. After some initial discussion, one brave man finally admitted his growing disgust: "This is pathetic. Is this the best we can do after all the teaching and preaching we've received?"

I had hit something raw and jarring. I had hit a divide inside of everyone else.

A PRIMER ON THE DIVIDED LIFE

The divided life is everywhere around us. We see it in the way parents raise their children and in the way husbands treat their wives. We see it in the way leaders lead and in the way followers follow. We see it in the way managers handle their subordinates, the way teachers handle their classes, the way friends handle their friendships. We see it in conflicts and misunderstandings, jealousies and cynicisms, pretenses and power struggles. But the clearest place we see it is in ourselves.

What exactly is this divide? It's the gulf between the human head and the human heart. It's the split between what we say we believe in our minds and what we really believe in our hearts. It's the chasm between our knowledge about God and our experience of Him. It's the gap that was exposed in that class I mentioned earlier, exposed perhaps for the first time for many. That's because the divide largely remains hidden, laced with the shame and fear that give the divide its terrible power and sway.

But there is another reason why this divide seems so pervasive. If it truly is this destructive, this crippling, we should all take notice and actively strive against it. But that's not what happens. The divide remains so gaping because we're used to it. We accept it as inevitable. It's just the way things are.

This condition sounds a lot like the sci-fi scenario portrayed in the film *The Matrix*. Here humanity lives in a computer-generated dream world run by artificial intelligence to keep humankind enslaved. Everyone is so used to the holographic fabrication presented to them that no one bothers to ask if it's real. No one cares to ask if there is something more. Everyone in the Matrix goes along with life, despite it being all lies, manipulation, and bondage. Similarly, we are often so busy surviving and getting on with life as it's presented to us that we never stop to ask, "What is this divide? Why is it there? What would life be like without it?"

But the issue is much broader than what was surfaced that day in my class. It's not just a struggle among churchgoers. It's a part of the universal human condition, a conflicted life of competing passions and interests, of warring forces and pulls. We see this clearly reflected in the stories we hear and the movies we watch. So many of them chronicle an internal conflict in the main character, one that drives the plot along to some kind of crisis.

Anna Karenina, Tolstoy's classic novel, is the story of a Russian woman in a sterile marriage who comes alive while having an affair with a young, handsome military man. She is caught between what is socially expected of her in nineteenth-century Russian society and a terrible ache in her heart to feel loved by a man. The split widens and tears her in two until the only choice left is suicide. The classic film *Dead Poets Society* also portrays well the divide. Here we find the brilliant and influential teacher Mr. Keating inviting young men in his class to live out of their hearts, to seize the day. One student tries to do so, embracing his longing to be an actor, only to slam up against his father, who insists on him pursuing a real career of medi- cine and giving up the nonsense of the theater. This story also ends in a tragic suicide.

The animated film *Beauty and the Beast* opens by introducing Belle, a charming young woman caught between life in a small French town and the longings in her heart for adventure and love. Everyone thinks she's eccentric, that she should just accept her lot, yet she longs for more than this provincial life. She refuses to cater to those expectations, yet by doing so and by choosing to love the Beast, she risks her own life and the life of her father. In a similar vein, *It's a Wonderful Life* is the story of George Bailey, a young man who longs to live a life of adventure and break free of the confines of small-town Bedford Falls. He wants to see the world and do great things. Yet at every turn, his dream to escape is thwarted until he finds himself facing bankruptcy and ruin.

The divide is demonstrated from a slightly different angle in the action film *Indiana Jones and the Last Crusade*. Indiana has been chasing after the Holy Grail, the supposed cup from which Jesus drank at the Last Supper. He wants it only for the fame and fortune it offers. But when a Nazi general also chasing the Grail shoots his father, he now has to retrieve it, not as an archeological treasure but as a cup that could offer healing to his dying father. In a poignant line, the general exhorts Indiana, "It's time to ask yourself what you really believe." [2] Indiana has to face the divide between what he may mentally assent to about the cup and what he truly places his faith in.

That tension comes to a dramatic, visual climax when he reaches a chasm that must be crossed to reach the Grail, a seemingly bottomless canyon with no bridge. It's a leap of faith. He has to trust his life to the explicit instructions his father procured to retrieve the Grail, that only a leap here would prove a man's worthiness to gain it. In this moment of terror, he decides to trust and steps out into the void, only to have his foot unexpectedly find solid ground. It's a bridge he couldn't see as long as he stood at the edge; only by his stepping out did it become visible. Indiana crossed the chasm by doing something counterintuitive. He couldn't bully his way through this in his usual manner—he had to trust. We will return to this important point later in the book.

What have you done with the split between what you have longed for and the life that seems handed to you?

This is but a smattering of examples of how internal conflict operates in the tales we know and love. But these stories are more than just stories. They mirror our lives, our struggles, our conflicts. Think for a minute about how the divide operates in you. How have you handled the gap between your head and your heart? What have you done with the split between what you have longed for and the life that seems handed to you? What have you done with your own disappointments, your crushed dreams? How do you handle what is expected of you in your family system? Is it freeing? Binding? What have you done with that? Where does it take you? What about expectations in the church or in society? What is acceptable to offer to others around you there? What seems unwanted or unvalued? What have you done with this? Finally, how do you present yourself to others? Is there a difference between the person you present in public and the one you live with in private? What is the difference? Why is it there? What's behind all this?

To all these disturbing questions, the Bible seems to add more trouble. Paul announced, "If anyone is united with the Anointed One, that person is a new creation. The old life is gone—and see— a new life has begun!" (2 Cor. 5:17). Yet for so many Christ follow- ers, the old seems to be hanging around relentlessly, despite all efforts to change. Was Paul guilty of apostolic hyperbole? Was he overstating his case to get everyone's attention? Why do the biblical truths that should comfort us seem so distant at times? Why is there often such a division between what we may read in the Bible and what we experience with our lives? Why the disconnect? What's behind this? The questions are unsettling. That's why we often choose to just keep moving. Perhaps in the busyness, we won't have to stop and face it.

THE CALL TO PUSH BACK

But this pattern of avoidance hits a snag when we look at the life the Scriptures call us into. While the Bible acknowledges in so many places the reality of the divide, it doesn't accept it as inevitable. The divide, from Scripture's point of view, is the abnormal, the deviant— it's not the way things should be. It's a split that needs to be mended, a tear that needs to be healed, a gap that needs to be closed. Throughout the biblical drama, we are being called to push back against the divide. We are being called to a life of single focus, of being undivided, of having one passion.

The psalmist, in an outpouring of triumphant faith, exclaimed the cry of his heart: "I am pleading with the Eternal for this one thing, my *soul's* desire: to live with Him all of my days—in *the shadow of* His temple, to behold His beauty and ponder His ways *in the company of His people*" (Ps. 27:4). It is the one desire that overtakes and consumes all others: he simply wants to be near God. But isn't this a bit of poetic license? Isn't he being caught up in the emotion of the moment? After all, what do we do with all the other things we seek after—approval, recognition, security?

But the same idea crops up in another psalm, in even stronger terms. The author was wrestling through the temporary success of the wicked when he came back to a confident trust in God, bursting out, *"For all my wanting,* I don't have anyone but You in heaven. There is nothing on earth that I desire other than you" (Ps. 73:25). A part of me looks at this verse as picturesque poetry, powerful to quote, even interesting to ponder. A different part of me objects to the whole idea: *Desire nothing on earth but God? But I long for so many things the earth seems to offer. I hunger after open landscapes and warm conversations, for music that enchants and mountains that beckon, to bask in the strength of men and enjoy the beauty of women, for times by the fire with Heidi and my daughters, for a hard workout on my bike and a good dinner afterward. I really do want all of these things. What am I supposed to do with these longings? Forget about them and just long for God?* But a final part of me doesn't protest. I'm curious, even intrigued. What would it be like to feel whole, to live undivided and focused? What would that look like?

Turning to the New Testament, we find Jesus underscoring the same idea in His interactions with two sisters, Mary and Martha. Jesus had come to stay with them and use their home as a base for His ministry. Martha was anxious and consumed with all the practical details that needed to be considered. She may have been concerned with how to feed and house the Master and His twelve companions. Perhaps she was worried about the house being clean and tidy for the wave of guests she knew would be coming to hear Him. But her sister, Mary, simply sat and listened, absorbed in Jesus' teaching, mesmerized by His presence. Martha's irritation at her sister's apparent indifference and laziness boiled over as she complained to Jesus. I imagine she expected Him to rebuke her sister and get her up and moving. Instead she got this: "You are so anxious and concerned about a million details, but really, only one thing matters. Mary has chosen that one thing, and I won't take it away from her" (Luke 10:41–42).

But again, we are left with more questions than answers. If the one thing is listening to Jesus and seeking Him, does this mean we stop attending to all of life's demands and just sit in His presence?

Throughout the biblical drama, we are being called to push back against the divide. We are being called to a life of single focus, of being undivided, of having one passion.

But that's totally unrealistic. Isn't this another case of dramatic overstatement?

Yet Jesus drove the same point home in His teaching. He instructed His followers not to be consumed with anxiety over money, even over basic necessities like food and clothing. Instead, we are to trust that the Father knows our needs and is going to take care of us, just as He clothes the flowers and feeds the birds. We are then to demonstrate that trust by seeking one thing above all others: the Father's kingdom and righteousness (Matt. 6:33). The kingdom is to be our central longing, our undivided passion.

Again, this sounds quaint. It makes a nice wall hanging, but to actually go here is another matter. What would it look like to have the expansion of God's kingdom be the driving desire of all we do? What would it mean to be that centered, that focused, so that we become unconcerned about our next day's food?

Just how far I was from such a reality became painfully clear on a recent backpacking trip with my friend Jeff. We had intended to resupply with food near the halfway point of our four-day hike, but when the trail intersected the highway where the store was supposed to be, we found that it had been shut down several years earlier. My friend took out his remaining food and suggested that we press on. He felt he could make it on rationed supplies, but I could feel the fear rising up in me: *What if I run out? What if hunger overtakes me?* And I had more food left than he did. With that kind of fear at hand, how can I possibly enter such a life as Jesus intends?

Yet the apostle Paul pounded out the same message with statements like: "For my life is about the Anointed *and Him alone.* And my death, *when that comes,* will mean great gain for me" (Phil. 1:21). And he pressed his point further in the same letter: "I now realize that all I gained *and thought was important* was nothing but yesterday's garbage compared to knowing the Anointed Jesus my

Lord" (Phil. 3:8). Again this strains credibility. All things are yesterday's garbage? Perhaps this was something for the apostle, but for us? What are we to think of our children and parents? What are we to do with our vacations and vocations? What are we to think of our hobbies and schools and dreams for the future? All of these are garbage compared to Christ? But Paul did not let anyone off the hook. Later in the same letter, he simply stated: "Imitate me, brothers and sisters, and look around to those already following the examples we have set" (v. 17).

The Bible has another way to put all of this. The life of single-minded devotion and undivided commitment is a life of purity. It's a life of holiness. Again the Bible is replete with commands using this kind of language: "Create in me a clean heart, O God" (Ps. 51:10). "Do all things without complaining or bickering with each other, so you will be found innocent and blameless" (Phil. 2:14–15). "Be holy, for I, the Eternal your God, am holy" (Lev. 19:2). "Since the One who called you is holy, be holy in all you do" (1 Peter 1:15). Danish philosopher Søren Kierkegaard summed it up well in the title of one of his books: *Purity of Heart Is to Will One Thing*.

Knowing all of this is a necessary starting point, but in the end it doesn't help very much. Remember, the class of adults I taught that day were well versed on the need to be pure and single-minded. They probably could have quoted some of the verses I just mentioned. But by their own admission, they were terribly divided. Something wasn't connecting. Something wasn't working.

A SHOCKING REMINDER, A SOBERING EXAMPLE

Even now as I write, I am startled by a terrible irony. I was just using a Bible reference book to look up the verses in the previous section. It was a birthday gift from a woman who had become a friend to our whole family. One day, she found her way into one of my classes at church and wanted to speak with me afterward. As her eyes began to fill with tears, I knew there was some terrible misery surfacing from underneath her usual happy demeanor. But all she could get out were generalities about the difficulties she was facing. Nothing specific was forthcoming. Concerned, I asked her, "Are you talking to others? Do you have friends who are walking with you?" She assured me that she did, mentioning a few names, one of whom was a pastor.

I left feeling that she was in good hands—but I soon found out it was all a lie. Those very friends she had mentioned to me were ones she had also kept at bay with generalities and half-admissions. Here was a woman who was sinking into crushing depression, who was living a divided life of secrets and unbearable pain. All she knew to do was keep running. But the running finally stopped when she took her own life a few weeks after our conversation, shocking the entire community who enjoyed her endearing personality. How could this happen to someone immersed in the Bible and in a community of believers? It's a question that haunts me now as I look at her gift of this book. How could such a thing happen? She was a divided woman, and the divide split her in two and then swallowed her whole.

Her tragic end is a brutal reminder of what can happen if we let the divide persist. It's not just an irritating feature of human existence or a life the Bible opposes. The gap between the head and the heart is a sickness, a disease, a cancer. It can take us all out—and it will if we let it. But how much are we willing to press in here? How much do we really want that purity of heart and single-minded passion? To what lengths are we willing to go to end the division and fragmentation? What are we willing to sacrifice?

Dean Potter is the nephew of an older couple my wife has known all her life. He also happens to be one of the greatest rock climbers in the world, noted especially for his exploits in free climbing—rock climbing with no ropes, no belays, no safety nets, just you and the rock and hundreds of feet of air below. To give you an idea of Dean's accomplishments, he has free-climbed El Capitan, a monolithic rock structure towering three thousand vertical feet in Yosemite National Park. Watching video footage of him as he works his way up any rock face is just mind-bending. One slip, one wrong move, one missed handhold, and it's death.

But even more spectacular are his feats of slacklining. Here he gets out on a line strung between two high points, sometimes hundreds of feet in the air, and just walks across it, much like the old tightrope walkers. When he loses his balance and falls (which he does), there are no safety nets below. He just catches himself on the line with his arms and slowly gets himself back upright onto it. Watching him perform this way can make me feel queasy, the way I do when I get to the edge of a cliff. Again, one bad error of judgment, and it's over.[3]

Dean is in his forties now and has been performing these stunts a long time, staring down death over and over again. The question that surfaces in my mind, in probably everyone's mind, is pretty obvious: "Why? Why push the limits? Why go to such extreme measures? Do you have a secret death wish? And what is going on in your mind as you do this?" He has been asked these questions before, and here's how he answers them: "When my life is at stake, I have an immediate focus. Focus or die."[4] And then he describes how this kind of razor-edge focus at first shuts down all perception, all feeling, except the rock or the slack line. But then it opens him back up to feeling connected to the world and to others in a way he can't experience by any other means.[5] It's the only time he feels centered, undivided, whole. Everything else drops away. There is a oneness of heart and mind. I have heard this same idea expressed in various forms by other mountain climbers and risk-takers. It's not a secret death wish; it's about feeling focused, undivided, at peace, even free. And if pushing themselves to the edge of death is the only way to get it, it's worth it.

His words are sobering to me, evocative of what I long for, of what we all should long for. He is willing to die to be whole. What are we willing to do?

PRAYER:

God, I come to You as I am, divided and confused, believing that You are there and yet so often feeling distant from You. I am not the person I want to be, or the creation You had in mind. So much is fragmented, flawed, broken, split. I want to be whole. I want to be a new creation in Christ. But I have no idea how to get there. I don't even know the first step. Guide me forward here. I am willing to go because I don't want to stay where I am. Even the unknown is better than the divided life I know now. Give me a wholehearted passion for You and Your kingdom. I believe You hear me and will answer me.

GOD: *Come as you are. You do have much to learn, but I am a patient teacher. Submit to Me all that you know of your head and your heart. I love to take what is split and heal it, what is broken and mend it. Trust Me on the road ahead even when it costs you. It's a good road because I am bringing you to Myself.*

QUESTIONS FOR JOURNALING AND DISCUSSION

These questions can be used in several ways. When they are used for private journaling, they can be a real help in learning to listen to our hearts. When they are used for small group discussion, they can help us listen to others, allowing the stories of our hearts to be told and heard. Finally, both of these ways can be combined so that a small group can spend time in journaling and then discuss what they wrote.

It is also important to note that these questions are suggestions, not mandates. If a question doesn't apply or doesn't seem helpful, skip it and move on. The important thing is that the deeper waters of our hearts get sounded, pulled up, and given words.

1. Did you identify with any of the stories told in this chapter, either real or fictional? With what exactly did you identify? Do you have any idea why you connected there?

2. How do you experience the divide between the head and the heart? Go to the list of questions posed near the end of the section "A Primer on the Divided Life." Choose a couple of questions that seem pressing or painful to you and seek to answer them.

3. Following are some of the responses that others had regarding their own personal core beliefs and commitments. Which ones resonate with you? Try to write one or two of your own.

   "If I speak up, I'll look like an idiot."
   "If I'm good, nothing bad will happen."
   "No one really cares what I say anyway."
   "If I stay disconnected, then I won't have to deal with people who hurt me."

"If God really loved me, this wouldn't be happening to me."
"Why try? Nothing will change anyway."

4. Read Psalm 73:23–25. This is an Old Testament picture of an undivided life. What draws you or intrigues you about this life? What puzzles you or confuses you?

5. Read Philippians 3:7–8, a New Testament picture. Again, what draws or intrigues you? What puzzles or confuses you?

6. What was your reaction to the two stories in the section "A Shocking Reminder, A Sobering Example"?

SURVEYING THE WRECKAGE

We have all lost touch with life, we are all cripples, every one of us—more or less.

—Fyodor Dostoyevsky [1]

It was time for the Sunday sermon, and I was the one to give it. The church had recently lost its pastor and had asked me to fill the pulpit that morning. Yet as I rose to speak, I felt unsettled, not from a fear of speaking but from something else gnawing at the edges of my consciousness. I don't remember anything I said that day. What I distinctly remember is that what I was saying had nothing to do with what I was feeling or thinking inside. I was a divided man. How did I come to be this way?

Just a couple of years earlier, I had left the pastoral ministry and had begun teaching Bible at a Christian school. It had been a time to come to terms with the inner messiness I had been running away from for years. The incessant fleeing had left me gasping emotionally and chronically depressed. There had been days I didn't want to get out of bed. At other times, connecting to others was such work that it seemed easier to stay alone. And then there had been those toxic moments when my darkness would erupt in anger, especially at Heidi or my two daughters. To stem the downward plunge, a psychiatrist had suggested antidepressants. I was at first resistant, but seeing my life spiraling out of control, I needed to try something different. So I gave in and, to my surprise, found the medication helpful, leveling me out, giving me the capacity to take stock of things.

During this period, like so many other teachers, I had to make extra income to supplement my salary. Besides painting and tutoring, I also filled empty pulpits. An understood honorarium for speaking became another way to make ends meet. So when I received the phone call from this particular church, I readily agreed. As Sunday arrived, I tidied up the sermon notes, got ready to leave, and took my medicine. As I said good-bye to my family, Heidi and I were struck by the irony of the situation: taking an antidepressant before standing in the pulpit.

Yet as I began to speak that morning, the irony shifted from the surprising to the disturbing. I felt distant from the congregation, as if they were seated in a huge stadium while I was on a platform

I saw clearly for the first time the deep divide in me. But what made it even more disturbing was this: I had no idea what to do about it.

hundreds of feet removed. The sea of space between us felt yawning, unbridgeable. A defining image then took shape in my mind. I saw myself wrapped in layer upon layer of gauzelike material, speaking out from under it in a muffled voice. The minister I projected outwardly spoke correct theology and sound biblical ideas, but the real man lay hidden somewhere underneath all that gauze, the man my listeners didn't know, the man *I* didn't even know. I felt divided from my hearers, divided from the truths I was proclaiming, divided even from myself. Perhaps the congregation thought the sermon was instructive or even inspirational—all I know is that I felt like an impostor. How did this happen? How did I get this way? And then I realized who had wrapped those layers of gauze around me.

I had. I saw clearly for the first time the deep divide in me. But what made it even more disturbing was this: I had no idea what to do about it.

SURVEYING THE WRECKAGE

Anyone who lived in the Middle Tennessee area remembers the great flood of 2010. We still tell stories about it to each other. More than thirteen inches of rain fell in a two-day period, sending creeks into basements and rivers into shopping centers. Gaylord Opryland, the largest hotel in the area, was submerged under ten feet of water in places. The basement of Nashville's multimillion-dollar symphony hall was completely flooded. Whole neighborhoods were swallowed in the surging torrent as rivers crested at record levels. I remember seeing one of the more shocking scenes on live TV news. A portable school building and an eighteen-wheeler truck were caught on camera, floating together down one of the interstates, now a rushing rampage of water. Our own home was threatened, as the floodwaters from the nearby Harpeth River backed up into drainage pipes and rose into our backyard. Had it rained a few more hours, we would have been flood victims ourselves.

But the worst part wasn't the flood—it was the devastation left behind. Mud-soaked homes and condos were everywhere. Up and down streets, homeowners pulled out furniture and possessions to salvage what they could. It looked like a war zone.

One afternoon I went to help clean out a student's home where the waters had risen eight feet inside. Most of the family's belongings were destroyed, and little could be saved. It was pathetic watching the daughter in tears, trying to pull apart rain-soaked family photos, hoping to dry them in the sun. The destruction was staggering. Our family would often walk to the swollen Harpeth, now several hundred yards wide in places, to view firsthand the flotsam racing in the current: whole trees, soccer balls, dead animals, remains of fencing, shoes, patio furniture, and trash everywhere. We were doing what everyone else seemed to be out doing, gawking at the sights, surveying the wreckage, keenly aware of the historic nature of this flood. Others whose homes were destroyed had an additional task: slogging through the muck, assessing the damage, and starting the cleanup.

What we face with the divide between the head and heart is something like this. It is a catastrophe of colossal magnitude, a shattering of the human psyche from which no one is exempt. But the worst part isn't the damage; the worst part is our usual response. With wreckage strewn everywhere around us and in us, we don't lift a finger. We think this is just the way life is. Imagine such a response from those whose homes had been ransacked and destroyed by the flood. It would have been an invitation to despair. But the flood was not the norm. It destroyed the norm. Only as we come to see the divide in this way will we be prompted to enter the muck and begin the cleanup. But what is the muck we must enter here? What is the actual wreckage? Perhaps the best way to start is with something universal, something with which we all easily identify, something I call the Grand Masquerade.

LET THE MASKING BEGIN

What is the Grand Masquerade? It's the universal compulsion to hide, the commitment to mask our true selves. It often begins in adolescence, when the feelings of shame, fear, and social expectation erupt with venomous force. In my years as a high school teacher, wearing the mask was a constant point of conversation with students. *Why do we do it? What is the obsessive pull behind it?* But their reaction to it in others was more troubling. They universally hated the mask when they sensed others wearing it. *So why do we continue to do it ourselves? What is going on here?*

What we are experiencing is a global cover-up, a Grand Masquerade. At some visceral level, we all believe that we are unacceptable to others, that if we disclosed our truest self, we would be rejected, mocked, and then abandoned. The dread of that exposure is so overpowering that we split ourselves in two, projecting outwardly something we hope will bring us affirmation, while inwardly hiding our shame-filled core. As we choose to linger at the masquerade, we become increasingly expert at constructing masks, at image management. What I was feeling that Sunday morning in the pulpit was just an advanced state of the cover-up. After doing it for so long, it was finally catching up to me. The gauze was no longer a covering; it was a death mask, and it was suffocating me.

One friend tells the story of how he found a way as a boy to get the affirmation he so lacked. When he would interact with adults, especially women, he would act serious and wise in their eyes. It brought him connection, but more important, praise. He was lauded as a boy mature beyond his years. As he got older, this habit progressed into a demand for deep conversations, especially with the girls he dated. Going out for fun never crossed his mind. Further, as a basketball star, he was lauded for his accomplishments, and that kind of affirmation kept him playing hard, hungering for more. But the real man, along with the sadness of his story, was locked away in a closet, unavailable for public viewing. The divorce of his parents and the growing depression he felt seemed to have no place to come forth. He had to keep running. He had to keep hiding.

Another friend of mine came from a quiet, dutiful father and a depressed mother who doted on his outward appearance. His life became one long tale of window-dressing, trading images to offer what seemed to make life work. He offered his athletic skills to high school coaches and his striking looks to women. As he entered the working world, he offered his sales ability to the corporate world and his natural charm to garner clients. He became so good at masking that others thought of him as the father and husband of the perfect family. But the window-dressing began to slip with a growing dependence on alcohol and a deepening unrest in his marriage. Only through the scraping pain of divorce and job loss did he decide to leave the masquerade. It was time to throw off the mask and dis-cover who was underneath. But as he started the dismantling, what he discovered was even more distressing: he had no idea who he was. This is where we all end up at some point.

But the Masquerade doesn't have to become apparent in tragic ways; it can show up in inconsequential moments. Recently, Heidi and I met several couples for dinner at a nearby restaurant. One of the women at the table was wonderfully engaging, yet when the conversation shifted to something personal in her life, I noticed something striking: she would turn her head. She couldn't make eye contact with me. I wondered, *Why did she have to turn away? What was she hiding? What was behind this?*

Our universal struggle becomes displayed in a metaphorical way in *The Phantom of the Opera,* in which the young man Erik is tragically burned and his face horribly disfigured. He feels like a monster and, ashamed of his appearance, he hides underneath the opera house in the sewers of Paris. Along with concealing his presence, he constructs a mask to hide his face. It is the only way he knows to survive his appalling situation. The pivotal moment comes when Christine, the opera singer with whom he has fallen in love, unmasks him and sees his terribly scarred face. He is exposed in all of his horror before the only person he ever dared to love. We connect to this story so deeply because it's our story. We all feel like monsters. We all cower in the sewers. We all construct masks to hide behind. And underneath lies the sleeping terror: *What if I am exposed? What if the mask is ripped off?*

It is instructive to note that no one has to teach us to hide. We are never given tutorials on how to assemble a mask or how to wear one. Somehow, beyond our understanding or control, we all receive invitations to the Grand Masquerade and feel compelled to attend. The thought of refusing the invite never occurs to us. Yet it is this very masquerade that ends up making life miserable, even unbearable. What in the world happened here? How did we get ourselves in such a deplorable situation?

PLAYING THE HYPOCRITE

But the damage of the Masquerade can be taken to another level, called *hypocrisy.* This becomes apparent in the derivation of the word *hypocrite.* The early Greek plays were limited in terms of makeup and cast. Further, only men were allowed to be actors even though women appeared in the script. They pulled this off by holding up different masks to their faces, depending on the roles they were playing. The actors themselves were termed *hupokrites* in the Greek language. It's not a big conceptual jump to our use of the word. Being a hypocrite is simply wearing a mask, pretending to be someone else. But now the mask is not just to hide or cover up. It's a power play, offering a sense of status over others, with an ability to push them down if needed. It can take on many forms, but the classic one is saying one thing in public and then behaving differently in private. When this is laced with religious language, it becomes especially repulsive. But our universal aversion to it is again revealing. We all hate hypocrisy. Why? Because we don't want to face it in ourselves.

The real devastation of it, however, comes out when we have trusted the hypocrite and are then crushed with reality. This is especially true in religious contexts, whether it's church, school, or even family. We are all looking for role models, for those who truly know God and walk with Him. We ache for heroic men and women, for leaders we can trust and pattern our lives after. The betrayal of that trust can be shattering.

One of my friends from seminary had his own crucible of betrayal in the church where he worked as an associate minister. One of the pastors was a powerful personality whose strong leader-ship invigorated the church and whose preaching was magnetic. He addressed the real issues of the heart, not the usual sermonizing. My friend was drawn to follow this man, for he seemed to know what he was doing and where he was going. But it was all a lie. The pastor turned out to be a fraud, a man more interested in grandstanding and applause than in seeking the kingdom of God. This all became apparent when he later left the church, divorced his wife, and abandoned his family. The aftershocks were heartrending. My friend was shaken, but the betrayal for others cut deeper, causing them to leave the church and even the faith.

There are many variations on this same tragic scenario. Consider this one: Karl was a spiritually sensitive boy growing up in Germany. When his Jewish father decided to move the family to a different town, he announced to them that they were all going to become Lutherans. It was better for business. The shock of this led young Karl away from religion and into the atheistic thinking of his day. Being gifted intellectually, he quickly took to these new waters and over time crafted his own philosophy, one that was to make him a household name. The philosophy was Communism; the man— Karl Marx.

John was another boy with a deep spiritual intuition and an instinctive love of nature. His father was a harsh and overbearing churchman who believed that anything except the Bible was frivolous. By age eleven, John had memorized the whole New Testament and even some of the Old, quite a feat for anyone, much less a boy his age. But the price tag was enormous. His father repeatedly whipped him until he got the verses right. The brutal hypocrisy of it all pushed John away forever. He walked out of the church and into the woods, never to return. He ended up becoming one of the great naturalists of his day. The man: John Muir.

It is the wreckage of souls that makes hypocrisy so egregious, so disturbing. It is the poison of the divided life spewing itself out on unsuspecting victims. Perhaps this is why Jesus' response to it is so

---

We ache for heroic men and women, for leaders we can trust and pattern our lives after. The betrayal of that trust can be shattering.

biting. He embraced the hated prostitutes. He accepted the traitorous tax collectors. He was patient with his witless disciples. But for the religious hypocrites of the day, he aimed all his verbal ammo: "Woe to you Pharisees, woe to you who teach the law, hypocrites! You traverse hills and mountains and seas to make one convert, and then when he does convert, you make him much more a son of hell than you are. . . . You are children of vipers, you *belly-dragging* snakes, you won't escape the judgment of hell" (Matt. 23:15, 33). Jesus' rage was not just about the hypocrites themselves but about the terrible damage they were inflicting on others. Sadly, the damage continues today.

LIVING IN A DOUBLE WORLD

The universal masking can take another form besides hypocrisy. It's a split entailing a more complicated cover-up with a more intricate set of lies—for now we are not just masking; we are bisected into a double life. It's Dr. Jekyll and Mr. Hyde come to life. One side poses as the real person, with whatever facade is needed to maneuver through accepted social and religious expectations. The other side is riddled with some dark secret or addiction, entangled by shame and fear. The divide grows deeper as the addiction pulls tighter and the facade struggles to keep up. Unlike hypocrisy, the double life can rarely be maintained long-term. At some point, the secret life storms out to take over or stumbles out to cry for help.

One of the best visual presentations of such a double life was the movie version of Johnny Cash's life, *Walk the Line*. Johnny's shameful trauma occurred as a boy when his older brother died in a lumberyard accident. In a drunken rage his alcoholic father blamed him for his brother's death, yelling out, "The devil took the wrong son." It was like a shotgun blast to Johnny's heart, a wound that mercilessly bled him for years. With his budding musical talent as a young man, he found an open door into country music, but his shameful past kept surfacing as anxiety, only slightly lessened by pills and alcohol. Thus began Johnny's descent into substance abuse. On the outside he was a rising star in the musical world, playing around the country to adoring audiences. On the inside he was increasingly chained to his addiction, more violent, more restless. The double life destroyed his first marriage and then began corrupting his career, as he became more and more confused and unpredictable onstage. The change came only when he admitted his double life, got off the drugs and alcohol, and came to Christ.[2]

Again, this type of story can be played out in so many ways. A student once confessed to me his habit of drinking and partying. As he told his story, he related a surprising insight. Although he knew that the alcohol had its own set of problems, the worst part for him wasn't that. It was the double life. His daily existence revolved around the next chance to drink, usually in some hidden or guarded spot. He lied to his parents at home and struggled to maintain his image at school. But at some point, the thrill of it all wore off and the double life became exhausting. He came to a Bible study at my house one evening and was struck by Jesus' call to come and find rest. It's what the double life had stolen from him, rest. That's when he realized he wanted out and came to me with his story.

I knew of another exceptionally bright girl whose academic performance was exemplary in high school. But to handle the stress of the expectations she felt, she became a private alcoholic, a secret she tried to hide from everyone until her erratic behavior became obvious her senior year. Only then was she able to get the help she needed. Another student I knew lived a secret life of porn addiction to jolt him out of the perpetual depression he wrestled with. After getting help and coming clean, he decided to do something else. He told his story to the entire high school during an assembly. The response? Other young men came up to him afterward, admitting their own double life with pornography.

In all of these stories, it is the pull of the addiction and the terror of exposure that severs us in two. We think we can hold it together, but we are deceived. Eventually the double life will come crashing down on us.

SPLIT BY SOCIAL EXPECTATION

The destruction of the divided life can come out in yet another way. It's not the hiding to which we universally succumb; it's the drive to fit in, the other side of the coin. Think about the last time you entered a new social situation. What were you thinking? Was it this: *How can I move into these lives? What do I have to offer? How can I enjoy them and allow myself to be enjoyed?* Sadly, it sounds absurd to imagine that possibility. Didn't your secret thoughts go here instead: *How am I doing? How am I looking? What is expected of me? Will they like me if I offer that?* It is this chasm between what we think is expected and what is truly in our hearts that creates the crushing tension.

Take Chris McCandless, the young man portrayed in the haunting story *Into the Wild*. Throughout college, Chris had succumbed to pressure from parents, school, and society to fit into a neat timeline of education, marriage, and career. But inside was a boiling cauldron of desire. He wanted to explore the world and test himself. He wanted to kill the old Chris that had lived under all the expectation and find his true heart. And kill it he did. Destroying all traces of his former identity, he spent two years wandering America, eventually ending up in Alaska. There he put himself through the final test: to survive out in the wilderness alone for four months with a bag of rice and a hunting gun. Sadly, it was this test that killed him, as he confused edible berries with poisonous ones in his search for food. Trying to escape social expectations cost him his life.

The weight of that pressure can come out in other ways. At the Christian school where I taught, we were always reminding students of God's love and grace, yet we could so easily succumb to the weight of what we thought others expected of us as faculty. The headmaster even admitted he used to put a heavy burden on the school, that when a senior walked across the stage at graduation he or she would be expected to be just short of perfection as a Christian. As teachers, we sometimes felt the same pressure, to look good as a school to parents and the community, but especially to the students. After all, we were supposed to be the role models. But the message students received from this posturing was very different: *Your inner struggles or doubts are not accepted here. You need to line up and look good like us.* The Christian life then became just another pressure to perform, and the necessary rules to keep order at school easily became confused with that life. Left unaddressed, it is this very tension that can cause students to jettison the faith once they leave for college. Who wants a life of pressure and rules?

This type of thing easily repeats itself in church environments. *What types of things are acceptable to talk about here? What things need to be kept under the carpet? How am I to present myself on*

Ironically, the one institution that asks us to admit our moral bankruptcy becomes the one place where that bankruptcy continues to remain underground.

Sundays? These types of pressures feel so strong precisely because they are so subtle. Often they are never openly admitted, and this only adds to their power. Believers unconsciously split themselves between who they are at church and who they really are. Ironically, the one institution that asks us to admit our moral bankruptcy becomes the one place where that bankruptcy continues to remain underground. It's no wonder that I have heard others tell me that an Alcoholics Anonymous meeting feels more like church than anything else they have ever experienced. For once the expectations were dismantled. The only expectation was complete honesty.

HEAD VERSUS HEART

The ancient conflict between the head and the heart has been noted since time immemorial. It is perhaps the most basic way the divided life shows up. Should we follow our reason or our emotion? Should we listen to logic or passion? It is the stuff that fuels the plots behind so many stories and movies. Jane Austen wrote a whole novel with this conflict in the very title, *Sense and Sensibility*. The Dashwood sisters are the main characters, each representing opposite sides. Elinor, the elder, is logical and practical, and lives out of good common sense—yet her inability to emote keeps her stifled and causes her to suffer. Marianne, the younger, is passionate and unrestrained, speaking out of her heart—yet living in the sensibility side of things gets her into endless trouble with others.

Stories like this leave us with many questions: *How are we to live, out of sense or sensibility? Or are we to live out of both? How do we do that when they conflict? Should we follow our passion for a new career that has great financial risk, or stay in one that offers security but kills our hearts? Should we follow a relationship that offers tastes of true intimacy, or stay in a marriage that feels dead? Should we speak what we really feel to others, or keep it under wraps?* We feel divided here.

And when the dividing involves walking with God, it is especially painful.

I remember one student who was so rational that he seemed robotic. During class discussions, his questions were always about the finer points of Christian doctrine, never about any heart issues or struggles. When he tried to enter into the banter of the moment or connect with others in the class, he looked confused, as if he didn't know how. He seemed to have a conceptual understanding of the faith, but no feel for it. One minister I worked with had a mother who died when he was a child and a father who was emotionally distant. Not having traveled through the grief of being disconnected from both parents, he simply became a Bible answer-man, to use his own terminology. He could spout endless theology on cue, yet he struggled to relate to others. His constant verbiage became a way to shield himself from the bleeding wounds of boyhood. But the payoff was tragic: his head had hijacked his heart.

But the hijacking can go in the other direction. In a striking parallel to the last story, another pastor I know lost his father in a tragic accident when he was a boy. His mother, unable to process the grief, simply disconnected, so he essentially lost both parents at the same time. The terror of abandonment and the need for affirmation then became massive undercurrents in his life. Becoming a pastor didn't solve those issues; it just intensified the pull. He struggles today with a compulsion to compare and compete with other pastors along with a fear of losing members of his own church. Yet he knows the truths of the Bible, that the Father will never abandon him and that he is deeply affirmed as a son in Christ. He knows these things and preaches them. Yet the pull to compare and compete swells up and crashes in on him at times. It trumps the truth he knows in his head.

My wife, Heidi, went through a very difficult time in early adolescence, struggling deeply with feeling unwanted and rejected at school. It left her with a message that something was wrong with her heart. The shame of those years can still color how she interacts with others. The fear of rejection can overpower the truth that she belongs to God, or it can lead her to misinterpret what she experiences from others. Even though she believes in her mind that she is treasured in the Father's sight, she still finds that the emotion of shame can overthrow and dominate.

READING THE BIBLE

Ironically, the one place that offers a cure for the divided life can end up being a place that divides us further. The Bible presents the enticing possibility of a life without division or fragmentation, and points the way to get there, through the separation Jesus experienced. He was divided from His Father, torn in two on the cross, so that we don't have to be. We are made whole by being brought near to God. The connection we feel with him now becomes the driving passion of our lives, healing our souls, shifting our motives, coloring our thoughts, altering our behavior.

Reading the Bible is a necessary start to understanding this possibility, but reading it in and of itself won't heal the divide. Studying passages and memorizing verses is also no guarantee. Even being a teacher or preacher of the Bible is no sure cure. For the very way we read and interact with the Bible often reflects the divide rather than heals it. How do I know this? It's the story of my life.

From the earliest days of my newfound love for Jesus, the Bible held a significant place for me. I tried to read it regularly throughout high school and college, even though there were lapses at times. But when I went to seminary, I saw the Bible in a new light. I clearly remember the first time I was able to read the opening of the book of John in the original Greek. I felt awe mixed with the excitement of entering the world of the Bible this way. I spent hours in my classes researching verses, diagramming sentences, writing out passages in Greek and Hebrew, reading commentaries. It became a place of endless intellectual stimulation. When I left seminary and entered the ministry, I would put hours of research into a sermon and then tack on stories and practical points to connect to my listeners. The result? I was applauded for my ability to teach the Bible, and that affirmation drove me to work at it harder. I was determined to get the Bible into the hearts of my listeners. It became a driving passion, a consuming quest. There was only one problem: I couldn't do it to myself.

Despite all my best intentions, I struggled to connect to the God I so passionately proclaimed from the pulpit. I struggled even more to connect to my congregation. I was a lover of the idea of God, not of God Himself. I loved the idea of loving others, but actually feeling it, walking in it? That was another matter. This is exactly where I found myself as I gave the sermon that Sunday morning, wrapped in the gauze that had become a straitjacket, one that was now suffocating me. You see, my life had recently unraveled over a failed church plant that I had pioneered. Remember the vow I had made to myself long ago: I would never fail in front of others. And now my worst nightmare had happened—I had failed as a church planter. I was angry with God for not coming through and ashamed of myself for not succeeding. And I had no idea where my life was going to go.

The very way we read and interact
with the Bible often reflects the
divide rather than heals it.

The emotional vertigo I experienced during that time left me disori-
ented, staggering. On top of that, my newborn daughter had medical
issues that would require additional surgeries to correct, and my
marriage was on the ropes. The inner turmoil and anger I felt
seemed like a black hole to Heidi, and she felt herself being sucked
into it. She pulled away from me, fearful and desperate herself. Even
now it is difficult to describe the darkness of those days. I felt myself
skidding into oblivion. There were even fleeting thoughts of ending
my life. Despite my extensive knowledge of the Bible, it did not
counter the black depression I had plummeted into or the crushing
shame I felt. In fact, it only seemed to make things worse. I could
teach all the truths that were supposed to help, but nothing seemed
to help *me*. Something was terribly wrong, but what? What was the
matter with me? Where was I to turn? How was I to keep from
drowning in the void?

My personal quest to know and teach the Bible had come to a
blunt dead end, yet I still desperately wanted to enter its truth. But I
now found the doors locked and the keys thrown away. Despite my
desperate banging, there was only silence. I was not going to enter
that way. I was going to have to find another path, and that would
require another quest, one that would change everything. It would
require not just knowing truth but entering a story. It would mean
facing things I had been running away from for a long time, things
we all run away from.

But that takes us to the next chapter.

**Despite my extensive knowledge of the Bible,
it did not counter the black depression I had
plummeted into or the crushing shame I felt.
In fact, it only seemed to make things worse.**

PRAYER:

God, You know my heart. You are so aware of my sin and my story. You know me more than I could ever know myself. You see the wreckage I have caused in my life. You see the deep divides and the misery and confusion it has caused. You know that I am limping through life. I have nothing I can offer you that is good, and there is nothing I can hide from You. If Your truth can put me back together, if Your Son can truly make me whole, if Your Holy Spirit can heal me, open the door, the door I can't even see now. I wait, hoping that You hear me.

GOD: *My child, I do know you. I do hear you. Believing that is how you will find the door. And when you find it, keep knocking. It will open.*

QUESTIONS FOR JOURNALING AND DISCUSSION

1. Do you remember when you started to attend the Grand Masquerade and wear a mask? How did it happen? How do you continue to wear one today?

2. How has hypocrisy in the church grieved you or wounded you? How do you play the hypocrite yourself at times?

3. How have you seen the double life in the stories of others? Is the double life a part of your own story? If so, how?

4. Do you feel a pressure to fit a certain mold in your school, workplace, church, or family? Take one or two of these social environments and describe the pressure you feel.

5. In the section "Head Versus Heart," with which stories did you identify? Which side seems to win the battle in your life? How does it happen with you?

6. "The very way we read and interact with the Bible often reflects the divide rather than heals it." React to this statement.

A TALE OF
TWO TALES

When Christ calls a man, he bids him come and die.

—Dietrich Bonhoeffer [1]

It's a story I have retold many times. It came from one of my former students, a young man with a bicultural background, his American father having founded a ministry in Africa. Living back and forth between the United States and the African continent gave him a unique perspective I grew to appreciate—but living in two different worlds also made him vulnerable to comic misunderstandings. One Sunday after going to church in South Africa, he and his family were invited to the pastor's house for lunch. After the meal and some extended conversation, the pastor suddenly announced, "I'm going to go have a little do-do." Shocked by such a statement, the young man just tried to ignore it—until the pastor's wife soon followed with the same suggestion: "I think I'm going to go have a little do-do also." Only later did he learn that *do-do* is a perfectly acceptable term in that culture for *nap*. Of course, such linguistic mishaps are funny and make a great story, but there are other things about living in two cultures that are far from funny.

In that culture, white Americans are associated with wealth and thus become targets for theft. That targeting became reality one day when robbers kidnapped the young man's family as they toured a neighboring village. Holding guns to their heads, the thieves seemed intent on stealing anything of value. The terror only increased when his father was separated out while the rest of the family was led back into a forested area. Typically in these situations, hostages are killed, but his father was able to remain calm and negotiate their release with money. They were allowed to go, but the scars of that event still remain with this young man.

Between the comic and the tragic, being bicultural was a daily challenge for him, with struggles that were hard for others to under-stand. He felt too American to be African and too much a part of Africa's world to fit into America's. Each culture had its own compet-ing narratives, with differing assumptions about life. In America, efficiency and improvement are prized. In Africa, it's all about rela-tionships and contentment. In America, the conversation tends to focus around what you are doing. In Africa, it's more about who you are. In America, when you meet with someone, it's for an hour, perhaps two, and then it's on to the next thing. In Africa, to meet with someone means that you spend the whole day with that person. As a student at both American and African schools, he struggled to maneuver through these two cultures, trying to blend in

---

Choosing which kingdom to live in radically shifts everything in our lives— our dreams, our choices, our lifestyles.

wherever he was, but never feeling that he belonged anywhere. Yet he has no regrets about his upbringing, for it has given him a distinct viewpoint with an atypical wisdom for someone his age. Taking a cue from Charles Dickens's well-known novel, we could call his story "a tale of two cultures."

But this notion of conflicting narratives can play out in other ways as well. Adolescents from divorced families often find themselves being traded back and forth between Mom's house and Dad's. What is prized in one home may be ignored or even scorned in the other. It can leave the son or daughter in a constant state of flux, always trying to negotiate between two contrasting expectations. We could call this story "a tale of two homes." I have also seen this same tension reflected in life at the high school level, as students struggle to find acceptance and identity. Solid grades and good behavior may be prized by teachers and parents, but athletic prowess and social standing seem to gain more respect with peers. Which story line should they choose? We could call this conflict "a tale of two identities."

When we open the Bible, we find a surprising parallel. It's the story of two competing narratives, both running throughout, and as the story unfolds, it seems that we are always being asked which one we want to live in. Long ago, the early church father Augustine rightly noted that the whole Bible is about two kingdoms: the kingdom of man and the kingdom of God. And choosing which kingdom to live in radically shifts everything in our lives—our dreams, our choices, our lifestyles. We could call the Bible "a tale of two tales." What exactly are these two tales, these two opposing story lines? And what does this have to do with our divided souls?

A TRAGIC NARRATIVE

The first tale is a grievous one of loss and ruin. It begins with a tragic act of unspeakable sadness. To go there is to return to the scene of the crime, for all that is deeply wrong about us can be traced back to it. The Bible opens with the story of creation, with all its wonder and beauty, as God Himself saturates it with His glory. It comes to a climax in the creation of man and woman. Adam and Eve were set in a lush garden, where they were free to explore and work, provided for at every turn. As the account unfolds, we feel the mystery of the tree that God asked them to avoid among the countless other trees from which they could eat. We feel the dignity of Adam as God let him name the animals, showing Adam's authority over creation. We feel the burst of joy when Adam broke out into poetry as he gazed on Eve for the first time. We feel their tender intimacy as we see them walking together naked, in a world where shame had no reality and fear had no sway. And over all, we sense the Father's delight in all He had made, a delight centered on this couple and the communion they all shared together. But all of that was about to be shattered. Into this utopia, tragedy struck:

> Now the serpent was more crafty than any of the wild animals the LORD God had made. He said to the woman, "Did God really say, 'You must not eat from any tree in the garden'?" The woman said to the serpent, "We may eat fruit from the trees in the garden, but God did say, 'You must not eat fruit from the tree that is in the middle of the garden, and you must not touch it, or you will die.'" "You will not certainly die," the serpent said to the woman. "For God knows that when you eat of it your eyes will be opened, and you will be like God, knowing good and evil." When the woman saw that the fruit of the tree was good for food and pleasing to the eye and also desirable for gaining

wisdom, she took some and ate it. She also gave some to her
husband, who was with her and he ate it. Then the eyes of both
of them were opened, and they realized they were naked; so
they sewed fig leaves together and made coverings for themselves. (Gen. 3:1–7 NIV)

When I lectured about this passage to high school freshmen,
I would take a glass vase and abruptly fling it against the classroom
wall, shattering it into hundreds of pieces. This is perhaps as good a
visual as any for this story. It is a shattering, a true tragedy in every
sense of the word, from which there seems to be no recourse. How
can a million glass fragments ever be made whole again? How can
what is shattered be put back together? It is the question that lingers
in the air. But before we approach any answer, I want to highlight
several important features from the story.

The first is a clarification. The real fall, the real crime, was already
happening before the actual taking of the fruit. We all sense that our
outward behavior emerges out of a stream of inner thoughts and
sensations that drive us to do one thing or another. Just this afternoon, I was considering whether to start a fire in the fireplace. I
thought about the warmth it would provide on a cold, rainy afternoon. I thought about how my daughter Rachel, now home from
college, would love to read by it. I thought about how Heidi would
enjoy a nap on the sofa next to it. But then I thought about the time
it would take to start, the rain and wet wood I would have to deal
with, and the effort required to keep it going. After a few seconds of
wavering, I made my decision. I got the wood and matches and went
at it.

This is a mundane example of what happens all the time. Our
outward behavior becomes a visual representation of our inner
realities, what we feel and think. The story of the fall is just another

instance of this, for the transgression was not just the outward eating of fruit. It was something already happening in Eve's inner world, the place where the evil one cleverly chose to assault her with his cunning lies. With the opening question ("Did God really say . . . ?"), he evoked in her an utterly new train of thought never before experienced: doubt. Eve's inner monologue may have run something like this: *I think God said not to eat the fruit. Or did He? Did Adam hear it correctly? Perhaps I heard Adam wrong. I'm not so sure anymore.* And along with doubt, fear usually comes as an emotional companion. The way we thought about the universe, the way we thought about a situation, the way we thought about someone, what if we've got it all wrong? With doubt and fear gnawing at her, Eve answered back with words she had heard from Adam: *No, I think that God told us we could eat from any tree we wanted to, just not that one.* Correct so far, yet she added something God never mentioned: *And come to think of it, we can't touch that tree either.* Her doubt and fear were already distorting things, making her see God differently. *Perhaps God is a little too restrictive; perhaps He is being a little too confining.*

Sensing her position weakening, the evil one went in for the kill. He openly negated what God had spoken: "You will not certainly die. For God knows that when you eat of it your eyes will be opened, and you will be like God, knowing good and evil" (vv. 4–5 NIV). The lie was not just a denial of the original prohibition. The deeper lie was how Satan portrayed God: as a grudging tyrant who wants to keep all the real treasure for Himself. So, instead of seeing God as a Father who enjoyed their presence and wanted them to enjoy His, instead of feeling safe and secure in this bond, Eve began to wonder now if God was hiding something from her with this tree. *Maybe God is holding out on us. Maybe He wants all the power and control for Himself. Maybe what I really want is on that tree.* As proof of her downward slide, she didn't run back to God and check this out with Him. She was already hooked to the lie: *God can't be trusted*. She had already begun to totter. The decision to pluck the fruit and eat it was just the final collapse.

Second, note what this lie was about. Up until this point, the story has described God pronouncing things good over and over again, six times about His creation and then a final "very good" after mankind was created and blessed (Gen. 1). God had also spoken about what is *not* good, that man should not be alone (Gen. 2:18), then giving Eve to him. It seems that God was providing the good for them at every turn, not keeping it from them.[2] But by casting doubt on God's goodness, the evil one offered her another option: *Take the fruit, the knowledge of what is good and evil, for you. You have to grasp this yourself, for God is not out for your good. You can't trust Him. You have to take matters into your own hands.*

Notice also that the fruit dealt with knowing something. Satan used this to cast true wisdom as something fundamentally different: instead of being known in relationship and exploring the world out of that posture, wisdom was now seen as grasping knowledge by one's own individual effort. And there the pernicious divide started to open. For the first time, Eve pictured God and the world as something to know, separated from herself being known. She disconnected from God out of fear, and in that isolation became convinced that the fruit was "desirable for gaining wisdom."

I remember feeling something parallel during my years at Duke University. My confusion and doubt about truth, about myself, and

---

There the pernicious divide started to open. For the first time, Eve pictured God and the world as something to know, separated from herself being known.

about God had escalated into torment. The questions would send me swirling down into an emotional labyrinth, where I would lose my bearings and disconnect from everyone. I had good friends, but my disengagement at times, even in the middle of conversations, earned me the nickname Airhead. They used it in a light-hearted way, but for me it was no laughing matter. One day I was walking through the Duke library, one of the largest university libraries in America, with floor after floor of books on every conceivable subject. The library was so immense that you could sit in parts of it and never see another living soul for the entire day. In that moment, I remember thinking, *If I could read all these books (or at least the important ones), perhaps I could finally solve the riddle of life; perhaps I could find the truth.* But after four years of constant pursuit and study, I was no closer to an answer. In fact, my attempt to know things in this solitary way only made matters worse in my inner world.

Something similar happened in the garden with Eve. She and Adam ate the fruit and their eyes were opened, but not to fresh wisdom about good and evil or further revelations about the world concealed from them. Instead, the revelation was about themselves. They felt stripped, raw, and naked. Disconnected from God, they became painfully self-aware. The repose of self-forgetfulness was lost, replaced by a jagged self-consciousness that now repeatedly cut and wounded itself. They were feeling the worst fallout of the shattering, something inconceivable up until that point. They were experiencing *shame*.

The repose of self-forgetfulness was lost, replaced by a jagged self-consciousness that now repeatedly cut and wounded itself.

Shame is the pervasive sense that something is deeply wrong with us, that we are unworthy to be seen and known as we are. Thus, we feel vulnerable before the eyes of others, eyes that could mock, judge, and condemn. As the first fallen emotion, shame is central to our core, a feeling so traumatizing that our instinctive response is to do anything to stop it. Adam and Eve reacted in just that way. They covered themselves as best they could with what were readily available—fig leaves. It must have been a pitiful sight. Gone was the possibility of being known, of trusting, of freely connecting to each other and to God. So was the possibility of feeling whole. What was on the outside would now conceal what was on the inside, something that had to be protected at all costs. The divide had split them further.

The tragedy deepens as the story continues. God came around again, walking in the garden in the cool of the day, looking for His prized creation. But instead of running out to meet Him, Adam and Eve ran away, hiding among the trees. Remember, shame demands this response: *Cover; hide; protect yourself.* But God called Adam out and questioned him about what happened. His response? Instead of coming clean and admitting his error, he dug himself deeper into hiding. He pointed the finger of blame at Eve and then subtly blamed God. When God turned to Eve to ask her about the incident, she just passed the buck to the serpent.

The ironies of the story are arresting. Instead of finding the good by eating the forbidden fruit, Adam and Eve found ruin and loss. Instead of becoming more like God, they became *less* like Him, facing decay and death. Instead of having their eyes opened to hidden wisdom, their eyes were darkened by shame and guilt. But as arresting as the ironies are, the divisions are even more startling. Adam felt separated from Eve. Eve felt the same toward Adam. They both felt cut off from God as He banished them from the garden. These relational divides only pushed the wedge of shame in further, cutting deeper into their inner core.

THE TRAGEDY REPEATED

The rest of the Bible is filled with stories of life outside of the garden, where the tragedy of the fall keeps repeating itself. There is Jacob, whose very name means "deceiver." He was the ultimate con man, manipulating others to get his way, until God showed up and wrestled him to the ground one evening to give him another name. There are the Israelites, rescued out of years of bondage to Egyptian rule. After a display of spectacular miracles, including unprecedented plagues, a parting of waters, and the daily provision of manna, they responded not with trust, but with grumbling and complaining. Some of them even suggested it would be better to go back to Egypt, where at least things were known and familiar. There is the tragic book of Judges, where the people of God repeatedly cycled through unbelief, idolatry, captivity, and deliverance. Despite God's repeated faithfulness, they chose to run away to other gods to cover their bases, just in case the Lord didn't come through for them. There is Saul, Israel's first king, who ended up being a power-hungry autocrat, always checking his approval ratings and obsessed with protecting his position, even if it meant killing David, his son's best friend. And then there is the litany of kings over both Judah and Israel, who, with few exceptions, refused to walk with God in trust and obedience. Instead they promoted their own reputations, making power alliances with surrounding nations and constantly dabbling in idolatry.

The New Testament gospels continue the same sad story line. The Pharisees were exposed as divided men, only interested in outward behavior and unable to connect with the life of the heart.

The disciples were constantly chided by Jesus for their miniscule faith. Even after watching Him do miracle after miracle, they still allowed fear and unbelief to rule their hearts. There is the rich young ruler, who wanted to show off his stellar moral record to the watching crowd. Instead Jesus exposed his inner corruption as a man who worships money. There is the prostitute at Jacob's well, who found her conversation with Jesus moving into perilous waters when He began to gently expose her sin. She wanted to debate theology as an intellectual deflection, but Jesus wanted to heal her heart. In all of these cases, we find the fall of man in some way recycled and repeated, the same tragic narrative over and over. The fear of exposure, the hiding, the control, the lack of trust, the rebellion against God, the deep divide—it's all there.

RECYCLED AND REPEATED AGAIN

But the Bible's stories carry such weight and power because they are the stories of our lives. In some way, we also repeat the tragedy of the fall. Without our approval, vote, or even awareness, we unintentionally relive the story of the fall, like a bad scene from a movie that gets stuck in a loop, replaying over and over again. One of my friends found himself in the second grade dealing with an alcoholic father and a sudden divorce. He couldn't process the abandonment, so he would spend his classroom time in the third grade daydreaming about having an NFL quarterback for a father and being celebrated himself as a football player. But as he went from boy to man, the daydreaming morphed into a life of running—running away from the shame of feeling unworthy and into anything that would make him feel alive. Like spinning in a revolving door, he succumbed first to alcohol addiction, then to a slavish commitment to his career, then to a compulsive devotion to sports and coaching, and finally to anything that would keep him distracted, anything to keep the shame at bay. The running continued even after a true encounter with Jesus that got him off the alcohol. Somehow, what he knew about Jesus was not reaching the deep places in his heart. He felt divided over what he knew to be true and the longings of his heart.

Another friend is a woman whose story begins with the aunt who raised her. Obsessed with exterior appearance, this aunt required everything to look perfect in her world. As a child, if my friend kept her bedroom tidy, she got verbal affirmation. If not, she got a frigid stare. But the standard neatness extended beyond the bedroom. She was locked out of the house every Saturday so she wouldn't mess it up. This rigid procedure was adhered to even during the brutal cold of winter. The only momentary reprieve was lunchtime, when she was allowed to come inside, but then left to herself to figure out what to eat. The compulsive devotion to externals also came out tragically in a lack of physical affection. Her aunt never hugged her or allowed herself to be hugged, explaining that it would mess up her makeup. My friend came away from her childhood with one very clear message: *To be loved, I must be perfect. Everything must be perfect, especially the way I look.* To lower this standard even a little meant opening the door to potential shame and criticism. When she came to Christ some years later, she heard about the love and affection freely offered to her by Jesus. But knowing this and feeling it were two entirely different worlds, worlds that seemed too far apart to ever be united.

My friend came away from her childhood with one very clear message: To be loved, I must be perfect. Everything must be perfect, especially the way I look.

My own story follows so many similar themes. With no older male reaching into my life as I entered adolescence, I collapsed into a story line of fear and self-protection, attempting only the things I knew would give me success. I became risk-averse. I jealously protected my heart. I felt smothered by shame. Yet even after experiencing the power of Jesus loving me during that time, I could never connect that saving power to the fear and shame that still haunted me. As I mentioned earlier, the divide only deepened in college, as I delved into various philosophical and religious systems, unsure of what was true anymore. It left my heart gasping for life, suffocating not just under the weight of shame but also under an increasing sense of despair.

In all of our stories, somehow shame and self-protection, unbelief and control, lead to division, unhappiness, ruin, and the curses of this life we all know and experience. As far as Adam and Eve are concerned, we are "chips off the old block," inheritors of their propensities, and yet responsible beings who choose the same path. Yet like Eve's choice, our decision to go down this path seems either perfectly reasonable or, more often than not, absolutely necessary to survive. But like Eve, we are deceived. And the deception comes to roost in the ruin we all make of our lives, in the tragedies we inherit and then keep repeating with our own tragic choices, in the terrible divisions we feel inside of ourselves and the terrible divisions we make in our relationships. If this were all there was to the biblical drama, we would only be left with a tragedy of Shakespearean proportions. But this is not the end of the story. This story is just the first tale. For there is another one in the Bible, another story being told.

THE TURNING OF THE TIDE

Every great story has a time when all seems lost, when the darkness and sadness of evil seem to have won the day. But that's not the end of the story. At the worst possible moment, something unexpected happens to turn the tide. Often it's the entrance of a certain character, a hero whose allegiance to something beyond self-protection and personal happiness turns the tragedy into a happy resolution. One only has to think of Frodo in *Lord of the Rings* or Luke Skywalker in *Star Wars* to see this at work.

This same pattern is exactly what we find in the story of the Bible. After the fall of man, Genesis tells the heartbreaking story of the spread of this ruin into families, nations, and the entire world. It even broke God's heart: "The LORD was grieved that he had made man on the earth, and his heart was filled with pain" (Gen. 6:6 NIV). But something happened to turn the tide, something unexpected in the story: a man named Abram, an idol worshipper from the city of Ur, is suddenly introduced into the narrative and given these instructions by God:

> **Eternal One:** *Abram*, get up and go! Leave your country. Leave your relatives and your father's home, and travel to the land I will show you. *Don't worry—I will guide you there.* I have plans to make a great people from your descendants. And I am going to put a *special* blessing on you and cause your reputation to grow so that you will become a blessing *and example to others.* I will also bless those who bless you *and further you in your journey,* and I'll trip up those who try to trip you *along the way. Through your descendants*, all the families of the earth will find their blessing in you. (Gen. 12:1–3)

In these few suggestive lines, we glimpse the contours of the second tale, a story of the undoing of the fall, the reversing of the curse, and the closing of the divide. This is not a tale of tragedy but of redemption, one with the sure hope of a happy ending.

First, notice who really turned the tide. Abram didn't step forward or even say a word. His only role was to be a receptive listener. It was God who initiated this turn of events, God who called Abram out into something dramatically novel and unknown. This is in stark contrast to the story of the fall, where Eve initiated the avalanche of ruin while Adam quietly participated. Left to our-selves, we will just add to the avalanche, but God comes to clean up the mess and set things right. He is the true hero of this second tale.

Second, look at the language. Without Abram's understanding or request, God simply came to bless. Five times the word *bless* or *blessing* is used in these three verses. What does it mean to be blessed? It means to be favored, to have the way opened back into a felt connection with God, to find His face turned toward us and His arms opened wide. God was inviting Abram back into a connection with Him. Only this kind of blessing can undo the tragedy of our lives.

Next, look at what this unforeseen favor meant for Abram. He was given a great role to play, one of beginning a great people, one that would demonstrate to the watching world what walking with God would look like. He also discovered in this great role that his own name and reputation would grow, that he would be a blessing and example to many. Instead of shame, he would find the oppo-site—honor and affirmation—but none of this came by Abram's ambition or control. It just came. Somehow the great thing that God was doing involved making Abram great along the way. It's an arrangement we are invited into also.

But the goal of this blessing was not just for Abram, or even for the nation to come from his lineage. It's for something bigger, some-thing so far-reaching that it seems impossible for Abram to conceive.

The goal of this blessing is the whole world. As far as the curse had spread its infection, the cure was coming to heal. For the story of the fall and the theme of all our fallen stories is one that is inwardly collapsing. Shame and unbelief set us on a course where we believe that the vortex of all reality always spins around us, sucking into itself everything nearby. During a recent summer cookout, one woman stated to me her conviction that everyone always has an agenda—that we are all trying to get something for ourselves out of every interaction. At first I wanted to disagree with such a sweeping statement. Yet when I thought about it, it seemed so true. The commitment to self-preservation, comfort, and power drives us to use others as tools in our private quest for happiness. This is always the agenda of fallen humanity. But in contrast to this inwardly collapsing story line, the new tale that God initiated is outwardly expanding. He began with Abram, then included his wife, children, and extended family, then pushed the boundaries outward into the future nation of Israel, and finally expanded it to take in the whole world.

But there is a catch. It was stated up front before the blessing was announced. To receive the blessing, to *become* the blessing, Abram would have to do one thing: he'd have to *leave*. This was not just leaving behind the customary idolatry he was raised in. It was not just leaving behind a few bad habits or character flaws. It was not even about leaving his house and moving to another part of Ur. This would be the utter abandonment of everything he had ever known:

Shame and unbelief set us on a course where we believe that the vortex of all reality always spins around us, sucking into itself everything nearby.

a decisive parting from his friends, his home, his culture, his religion—everything that felt safe, secure, and known. To make matters even more unsettling, no map or terminus point was given, no directions or advice for the road. All he was given is this: "Leave . . . and travel to the land I will show you. *Don't worry—I will guide you there*" (Gen. 12:1). It seems that the blessing could only be received by an experiential walking with God, learning to lean on Him every step of the way. Abram would have to give up all semblance of the known and step into the unknown. Instead of grasping at knowledge the way Eve did, Abram would have to let go and trust, being content that he was favored and known. This is the blueprint for the second tale, the one God is weaving.

Would you answer such a summons? Would I? Honestly, I don't know. What we do know is how Abram answered it: "*Without any hesitation*, Abram went. He did exactly as the Eternal One asked him to do" (Gen. 12:4). And with that leaving, everything changed. Isaac was born, the son of promise through whom the nation of Israel would eventually come. And through that nation, Jesus finally appeared, the Son of all the promises. And strewn throughout the Old Testament narrative, we have intriguing stories that taste of the blessing, ones of trust and obedience, not of shame and unbelief.

There is the story of Moses, who obeyed the summons to become the leader of an entire nation, even though he was plagued by self-doubt and poor oratorical skills. There is Joshua, who led the Israelites forward into the promised land. There he learned to trust and obey God's bizarre battle strategies, ones that eventually led to conquest. There is Ruth, a Gentile who exhibited an unwavering commitment to her Israelite mother-in-law and to the Lord, a commitment that, just like Abraham's, sent her away from her home, her culture, and her heritage. There is David, who slaughtered Goliath not just to win the battle but to let the whole world know that the Lord is the true God. There is Elijah, who put his life on the line as he exposed the false prophets on Mount Carmel with a demonstration of holy fire on drenched wood. There is Daniel, who refused to bow to idols, even though he knew it would mean death at the mouths of lions. And then there are the prophets, who obeyed God's summons and called Israel to repentance, often facing rejection and hardship in the process.

THE FINAL THRUST

But the final thrust of God's redemptive plan began in Nazareth, a country village so small and insignificant that it was a target of ridicule at the time. Ironically it was there that the story came to a climax. All that was revealed in the Old Testament would now get repackaged and redelivered in a strikingly original way—not in a message or in a miracle, but in a man. But this man was no mere man. The author of this second tale now walked onstage to play the lead role in it as Jesus of Nazareth. And what did this man do? He stated in no uncertain terms that there are only two tales to live in, only two paths to follow, and only two roads from which to choose. And in His teaching and conversation, He delineated the pathway of this second tale, one that leads us away from building the kingdom of man and into the new kingdom He is building. Then, like all good teachers, He didn't just talk about it. He did it Himself. He took the path He was asking us to walk down. What is this path? "If anyone would come after me, he must deny himself and take up his cross and follow me" (Mark 8:34 NIV).

In these few words, we have an outline of the final thrust, as opposite from Eve's agenda as could be imagined. Instead of control and manipulation, we find here denial and submission. Instead of unbelief and separation, we find trust and connection. Instead of knowing something, we are asked, like Abram, to walk into the unknown. And instead of shame and self-protection, we are asked to come and die. We are asked to enter the life of the cross. What is this life, and how does it help us become undivided men and women?

First, note the call into trust and connection. To "come after" someone was a common phrase at the time of Christ, used of a student who would pledge himself to a rabbi, to be trained by him and even live with him. It was to be a learner, a disciple. The whole feel of this path is one of life together with Jesus. It's about following Him, walking with Him, a communion of life and a fellowship of heart, something that Adam and Eve lost. But to place ourselves under Jesus' tutelage requires a risky obedience to His call here, a direct counter to the disobedience of the first tale.

Then notice the absolute submission required in the call. To deny oneself means to say no, to give up, to surrender. These are all opposite motions of the fall, where control appeared to be the more reasonable path, especially since God seemed neither control-lable nor trustworthy. But to deny oneself is not really about giving up this behavior or that bad habit. It's much more sweeping. This is a radical rejection of one's whole pattern of being. It's about giving up the manipulations and devices we have used to find life. It's letting all of that go.

In the next phrase, the denial of self leads to a decision to take up our cross. The denial of the old self has now gone one step further: execution. Its equivalence today would be to say that we must carry our own electric chairs on our backs. The idea is unset-tling, even shocking. Its angularity doesn't fit into our hidden hopes for a sensible solution to the divide. But there is even more here, for the cross at that time was no quaint religious symbol, as it is sometimes seen today. *Cross* was a word of such horror and shame that it was seldom pronounced in public. No form of death ever invented has been more cruel or torturous. The very act of dying on a cross was the worst form of humiliation, for those who died were often hung naked in public places to be gawked at. Adam and Eve maneuvered through the shock of shame by hiding and blame-shifting. But with the life of the cross, we find a refusal to protect ourselves, a refusal to cover, and a deeper dive into shame itself. How could this possibly be part of the healing? Yet Jesus still bids us to follow Him here into this perilous territory.

Finally, notice why we are to deny ourselves and take up the cross. All of this death is so that we can now follow Him. It's not a call into knowing a new idea or understanding a new philosophy. It's a call into knowing a person, of rubbing shoulders with Him so much that we start to become like Him. And again, as it was for Abram, it's a call into the unknown. For to follow means that we aren't leading, that we don't know the way, and that only naked trust will keep us on this path, leading us out of death into life. And just to remove all doubt that He was speaking the truth here, He did the unthinkable. He did it Himself. He denied Himself all the benefits and powers of being God in the flesh; He took up the Roman cross, suffering an agonizing death; and then He broke out of the grave to ascend back to the Father. And now he turns to us and says, "Come, follow Me. It's really true. This is the way. This is the path."

WHAT WE ALL LONG FOR

But even so, this leaves us with some very disconcerting questions. Why death? Isn't there an easier way to pull this off? Really, must it be so shocking, so dramatic? Can't we find something a bit more amenable to our tastes, a little more congenial to our sensibilities?

This has been a perennial problem, as generations have struggled to come to terms with Jesus here. But what if what He is saying is not something so offensive or loathsome? What if He is calling us into something that we secretly desire? What if the path He described is one that we long for, often without realizing it? I got my first clue about this from a totally unlikely place, a movie about Japanese warriors.

The tale of *The Last Samurai* centers around the journey of Nathan Algren, a dissolute and embittered US army captain in the late 1800s. Through a series of events, he takes on the job of teaching Japanese recruits how to fight using modern artillery and tactics. In so doing, he is preparing them to battle the fierce samurai warriors, whose refusal to renounce old ways are preventing the Japanese king from ushering his country into the modern era. But in the very first battle against the samurai, Nathan is captured by them and introduced to their revered leader, Katsumoto. As their prisoner, he learns the ways of the samurai, not only how to fight well, but to live well. From Katsumoto himself he learns the meaning of the word *samurai*, to serve. Here is the mysterious source of Katsumoto's strength and courage. This warrior has a higher mission than his own fame or glory: to serve the king for the glory of Japan.

The plot climaxes in a final battle scene, where Katsumoto chooses to charge the enemy's artillery on horseback, knowing it will mean certain death. But he would rather die serving the cause than go on living. After being repeatedly shot and mortally wounded, he

---

**To follow means that we aren't leading,
that we don't know the way, and that
only naked trust will keep us on this
path, leading us out of death into life.**

lets Nathan deliver the final deathblow with his own sword. As he dies in Nathan's arms, the opposing army looks on and then one by one goes prostrate on the ground out of respect and honor. They have just witnessed the death of a great man, the death of a hero.

Heidi had seen the movie and sensed that I needed to watch it too, so she gave it to me for Christmas. She was right. I did need to see it, and when I did, I wept. Here was a man I longed to be like, who chose a life of service rather than self-protection, a life of submission rather than control, whose very soul exuded a muscular reality, a strength on fire. Later, other realizations hit me. The path that Katsumoto chose was just an echo of the path Jesus had already pointed out. And my love for the hero Katsumoto gave me a new-found reason to love the great hero Himself, Jesus. Perhaps the life of the cross wasn't so offensive after all. Perhaps Jesus was telling me how to become the man I longed to be.

That door into the Bible, one of simply knowing its content, had already been slammed shut on me. But now, it was as if another door appeared, this one already opened. I didn't have to knock it down; instead, I was being summoned to enter. Yet as I stepped forward, I had no idea what I was entering or where this door would take me. It felt so unknown and uncharted. What I did not realize then was that this doorway was an entrance into the second tale. Neither did I realize then that entering it would begin the healing between my head and heart. I had just started the journey, and there was much more to learn.

Perhaps the life of the cross wasn't so offensive after all. Perhaps Jesus was telling me how to become the man I longed to be.

PRAYER:

God, so much of my life is caught in the web of the fall. I feel the pull of self-protection. I feel the fear of being exposed. I want to control rather than trust. I want to know rather than be known. I find myself manipulating others to get what I need. I follow old patterns that have long ceased to be choices and instead feel like ruts. I don't know how to change or even what I would change into. I am confused and lost. Yet, I want more. I don't want my life to be a tragedy. I want You. I want to be whole. You are weaving another story, and I want to be a part of it. I ache to be a part of it. I know that the entrance into it means surrender, risk, and death. I am afraid, and yet I am more afraid to stay where I am. Show me the next steps forward. I want to come alive to You. I want to be like Your Son.

GOD: *My child, I know your fear. I understand your confusion. I know your name. I love to take what is damaged and heal it. I love to take what is broken and mend it. I am making all things new, starting with you. Take whatever step you know you need to right now. I will lead you as you begin. Come forward into the unknown. It's where you will find Me.*

QUESTIONS FOR JOURNALING AND DISCUSSION

1. The story of the fall is the first tale of the Bible, a tragic narrative. Describe one or two new insights into this first story line that you gained from the chapter.

2. "In some way, we also repeat the tragedy of the fall. Without our approval, vote, or even awareness, we unintentionally relive the story of the fall, like a bad scene from a movie that gets stuck in a loop, replaying over and over again." Describe a couple of ways your own life feels like a repeat of the fall.

3. The blessing God gave to Abram begins the second tale in the Bible, a redemptive narrative. Describe one or two new insights into this second story line that you gained from the discussion on Abram.

4. The climax of the redemptive story is Jesus. He asks us to die and enter the life of the cross. This is how we enter this second story. What aspects of His call to die scare you? What confuses you? What intrigues you?

5. Describe a hero from a book or movie that echoes Jesus. What do you admire about this hero? What does your heart feel about the possibility of becoming like that person?

6. "Perhaps the life of the cross wasn't so offensive after all. Perhaps Jesus was telling me how to become the man (or woman) I longed to be." React to this statement.

PART II

TACKLING THE DIVIDE

Three Terrains to Navigate

> Thus I began: "Poet, you who must guide me,
>   Before you trust me to that arduous passage,
>   Look to me and look through me—can I be
>   worthy?" . . .
> So I hung back and balked on that dim coast
>   Till thinking had worn out my enterprise,
>   So stout at starting and so early lost.
>   —Dante[1]

It is one thing to behold from a wooded mountain peak the land of peace, but to find no way to it, and to strive in vain towards it by impassable ways, ambushed and beset by fugitives and deserters, under their leader, the lion and the dragon. It is a different thing to keep to the way that leads to that land, guarded by the protection of the heavenly commander, where no deserters from the heavenly army lie in wait like bandits.[2]
    —Augustine

Maybe the part that knows the waking from the dream, maybe it isn't here [the head]. Maybe it's here [the heart]. I need to believe that something extraordinary can happen.

—Alicia Nash to her husband, John, *A Beautiful Mind* [3]

> I will teach you and tell you the way to go *and how*
> *to get there*;
> I will give you good counsel, and I will watch over
> you.
>> —Psalm 32:8

SURFACING

*It is impossible to meet God without abandon,
without exposing yourself, being raw.*

—Bono [1]

"I hate cancer." Heidi utters this whenever she hears about a new victim of this scourge. I have grown to hate it also, what it does to the body, what it does to the mind, what it does to those who know and love the person afflicted. I watched my mother slowly succumb to it and my father-in-law quickly surrender to it. I have seen children orphaned by it and spouses widowed by it. I have seen limbs amputated and organs removed to stop it. I have even seen it take down young children who barely had time to know their names, much less their place in the world. And some of us have experienced the scare of something amiss in our own bodies. The ominous question jolts us with fear: *Is it cancer?*

But we are not defenseless against this foe. In the past few decades, remarkable progress has been made in the treatment of cancer: new drugs, new therapies, new technology. But the old wisdom still holds true: early detection is always best. It means you have more of a fighting chance to kill it before it kills you. But that doesn't mean the fight will be easy.

The battle strategy often involves cutting out the cancer and, if it all can't be removed, trying to kill what's left. But such a strategy involves inflicting pain, agonizing at times. Some chemotherapy will even bring the patient close to death in the hopes that it will be the death of the cancer.

My sister endured just such a strategy in her battle with breast cancer. After the shock of the initial diagnosis, she chose to have a double mastectomy in light of our family history of breast cancer. But the discomfort of surgery and recovery seemed mild compared to the agony of what was next: six rounds of chemotherapy every three weeks. With each injection of the drugs, she would begin a descent that felt like death. Because my sister was sapped of all energy, her very bones aching to the core, she was bedridden for more than a week each time. She said it felt like the flu times ten, but the worst part of it all was the headache. Until she found medication to help, she felt as if her head would explode. At one point while my sister was undergoing a CT scan, she broke down in tears, telling the nurse, "I don't think I can do this." But she did do it—and more—enduring not just six rounds of chemotherapy but six weeks of radiation treatment as well. The result of such a painful ordeal? She is now cancer free and back in her job as a pediatric nurse practitioner.

Every cancer patient goes through something like this. Yes, it's a shock to be diagnosed. Yes, it's painful to be treated. But it's far better than being taken down by the disease. My father-in-law lived

**We have to awaken to the sad truth that
we have maneuvered through life largely
based on lies we have swallowed.**

only seven weeks after his initial diagnosis. Why so quickly? It was pancreatic cancer, notorious for being asymptomatic until it's too late. He was oblivious to what was festering inside. That's why it killed him.

What we are facing in our souls is a similar prospect, for all of us have a cancer inside, one that is growing and festering, dividing our heads and hearts, splitting each of us into the person we project and the one we conceal. And it's slowly killing us. I wish I were exaggerating. I wish this were only hyperbole or hype. But everything I see around me, everything I see in me, screams the opposite—that it's true.

Recently I telephoned a man to discuss mutual ministry concerns. I told my story briefly to give him a bit of my background. Then it was his turn. He began with his father, a minister who had risen in the ranks of his denomination until he was one of its top leaders. His father's name was recognizable and his reputation unimpeachable. But all of that shattered when he was sixteen. In a moment of seeming insanity, his father abandoned his marriage and ran off with the secretary. It also shattered my friend, leaving him angry and embittered. How could a preacher of the gospel, a man entrusted with thousands under his care—how could he fling it all over a cliff, along with his wife and children, for another woman? He knew the truth. He taught the truth. Yet somehow his heart compelled him to choose another path. How could this happen? He was a divided man, and the divide took him out, along with his ministry and his family. This is no exceptional case, even if it was a more public one. I have seen this type of thing over and over in the men and women with whom I have worked and walked. The cancer is everywhere, brooding, lurking, malicious.

WAKING UP

If this really is our situation, we need to do something. Passivity or apathy will spell death. And what's needed is pretty straightforward. Like the unsuspecting cancer victim, we need to wake up to the cancer inside. It has to be revealed. It has to be surfaced. We have to awaken to the sad truth that we have maneuvered through life largely based on lies we have swallowed. Along with the wake-up call, we need to submit to the cure, one that always involves turning and facing the cancer from which we have been running. It's a cure that will take us into uncharted and dangerous territory. At times it will mean submitting to what feels like death, like emotional chemo-therapy. I wish I could tell you otherwise, but I'm afraid there's no other way. Yet we can draw courage from the pattern in Scripture. Remember Abram and his call to leave and enter the unknown. He did it and inherited the blessing. Remember Jesus and His call to come and die. He took the same path and came alive. That's where He wants to take us.

But choosing to wake up and submit to treatment poses imme-diate questions. The cancer patient has a doctor to diagnose the disease. How are we to diagnose ourselves? How do we surface the voiceless commitments, the unspoken vows, the lies and half-truths? How do we pull up something we are not even aware of? This sounds like searching for something lost, but you can't even remem-ber what it is, much less *where* it is. It feels hopeless from the start. Yet clues are dropped on us almost every day, clues that can open windows of revelation and unravel the mystery of our divided souls.

FOLLOWING THE CLUES

One of the best ways to begin this journey is by becoming attentive to our response to story, for a story can subversively bypass our intellectual defenses and connect directly into our pain and longings. Just such a moment happened as I finished reading *The Yearling*. It's the story of a boy growing up in the wilds of northern Florida near the turn of the last century. He was a single child with a stingy, frozen mother and a father the exact opposite, full of grace, humor, and love. The plot turns around the boy's adoption of a young deer he grows to love like nothing else, only to lose it tragically in the end as he becomes a young man. As I turned the last page, I burst into tears, all out of proportion to the reality at hand. After all, this was a fictional account of a boy a hundred years ago, in a setting with which I could hardly identify. So I stopped to consider my response. I then realized that I had connected so intensely with the story because I, too, had felt my heart as a boy lost forever as I entered the harshness of adolescence. My tears revealed to me that I still believed I had lost something that could never be recovered. And to deal with the seemingly irretrievable loss, I had hardened over the ache with passivity, niceness, even discipline. But the longing had surfaced again through the story. It felt as if I had grabbed a live wire that was supposedly disconnected. Perhaps my heart was not lost forever.

Movies can do the same thing. Just this week, I asked a group of men to talk about a movie that stirred something in them. As they took turns responding, I realized that I was feeling something of the real man surface in each of them, the one often locked away from view. This same deep stirring happens to me routinely with movies. I was stung by the loyalty and brotherhood portrayed in *Lone Survivor* as a group of Navy SEALs found themselves in a fight to the death. I was undone by *The King's Speech*, where a stuttering monarch finally finds his voice with the help of a mentor. And in the movie *Lincoln*, I was drawn to the greatness of this man as the story unfolded. When the assassination finally came, as I knew it would, I unexpectedly began grieving his death, for I had grown to love him despite his flaws. Each of these stories pulled out something in me usually hidden. They all awoke and revealed something that needed my attention.

But it's not just stories and movies. Everyday life poses many clues to our souls. The normal frustrations and disappointments can actually become places of discovery if we allow them. For instance, what is behind that constant impatience in the grocery store line? Or what about the fear that grabs you when the supervisor walks by your office? Why the anxiety about being late to a meeting, even if it's just a couple of minutes? Why do you feel such pressure when you walk into school or into work? Why the inability to speak and engage when your spouse becomes angry? What is behind the rage over the mess your child made while playing? Why the nagging compulsion to keep everything in order? What about your continual avoidance of a friend who keeps trying to contact you? Of course, nothing significant may be underneath—but then again, it could be a clue. You don't know until you stop and ask.

And then there are those repetitive thoughts that seem to be so much of our daily mental diet. All of us have a running stream of dialogue that we are constantly saying to ourselves, a kind of self-talk that we are so used to that we hardly notice it. In a counseling class I taught to high school students, I had them process on paper this running inner dialogue. What I got back in writing stunned me. Over and over, it was a conversation of self-abuse. I don't remember the exact comments, but here is the basic substance of those thoughts: *I will never be good enough to please everyone. Everyone seems to be happy but me. I just don't fit in here, no matter what I do. I hate my ugly face. I hate my body. I feel so much pressure to succeed. I wish I were somebody else. I'm always afraid my friends are going to leave me. If I don't have a boyfriend, I won't feel loved. If others knew what I struggled with, they would despise me. I always have to come through for everyone else; won't somebody come through for me? I hate the way I have to act happy all the time.* Thoughts like these can intrude into our own minds, a relentless stream of sewage drenching us with condemnation and shame. Just to put words to it is to reclaim some measure of power over it. But that's just a first step. Where in the world does this vicious onslaught come from? What lies behind it? The surfacing has begun even if the cancer isn't fully understood.

How we handle conflict can also be an important clue to follow. Do you sense conflict as a chance to break through to new levels of understanding? As a way to find a helpful compromise? Or does conflict feel like an attack from which you must defend yourself at all costs? What about those hard things you need to bring up with a close friend? Are you paralyzed by the possibility of rejection or hopeful about a resolution? What about your boss or superior? What if you disagree with the direction he or she is taking things? Do you voice your thoughts? Do you remain quiet in fear? Do you let your anger come out in a snide remark or a cold countenance?

What we do with conflict can be so revealing about what we really believe. It can also be unnerving. Recently at the dinner table, Heidi and I were reflecting on our growth and change in the past few years. I expressed that I had come a long way out of my self-preoccupied orientation. Heidi had a different take. She pointed out ways in which she felt that I was still fixated on myself. She felt I had actually been going backward, not forward. Rather than taking these

---

All of us have a running stream of dialogue that we are constantly saying to ourselves, a kind of self-talk that we are so used to that we hardly notice it.

conflicting views as an opportunity to learn and dive in deeper, I was engulfed in a firestorm of shame. I felt exposed, because deep down, I knew she had uncovered a continuing blind spot. And my old reaction to shame is one of vicious anger, either toward myself or toward those around me. This time, I erupted at her, telling her that I could not, would not, go back to my narcissistic posture, that I had fought too long and come too far to go back. Ironically, my passionate defense was only proving again my self-preoccupation. I was unwilling and unable in that moment to see things from her side, isolating her again, as I have done over the years. She was just voicing her heart, something I have longed to hear. But in my tirade, I wounded her again. Fortunately, we were able to stay engaged in the conversation long enough until we could confess our sins and hopes to each other. But I realized that something surfaced in the conversation, a reflexive self-protection still in effect, and with the one person who loves me the most. I knew there was more work to be done inside me.

And then there are the tragedies that descend on us. The sudden death of a parent, the loss of a steady job, the spouse who calls it quits, the car accident that leaves you permanently scarred, the child who gets hooked on drugs or becomes pregnant or commits suicide—all of these shake us to the core. In the rawness of these moments, what we really believe about life comes to the surface, often dramatically. In the Old Testament, Job had this experience, as tragedy after tragedy befell his happy and contented life. In the argumentative dialogue that ensued between him and his companions, Job revealed his core convictions. He believed that he had gotten a raw deal. God had treated him unjustly and cruelly, and if he could just get an audience with God, Job would show him just how wrong He was. What Job truly believed was surfacing. Part of the draw and irony of the book is that we find ourselves agreeing with Job, thinking his thoughts, feeling his argument justified.

Toward the end of the book (Job 38–41), Job got his wish—he got an audience with God. But instead of answers, he got more questions. Instead of being able to argue his case, God never allowed him the opportunity. Over and over God questioned Job about the mysteries of creation, the mysteries of this life, things that Job could never understand. By the end, Job had still gotten no answers to his predicament, but he got something else, something he came to believe was better. He got to experience God's presence and feel God's awareness of him. And that was enough, leading him to confess his arrogance and submit in repentance (Job 42:1–7). He still didn't know why the tragedies had occurred, and he realized that he may never know why. He never even learned of Satan's taunting of God, which actually precipitated the disasters, something we as readers know about. But it didn't matter anymore. Job felt that he had been noticed by God and attended to by Him. As the story ends, however, and his fortunes are restored, we can end up feeling, not resolution, but even more perplexity. *How could Job trust God again when He had allowed so much evil to invade his life? Job never got answers about anything!* Is this a reflection on the artlessness of the story's author, or is it more a reflection on our pervasive suspicion of God and our unfamiliarity with His presence? What does this story bring to the surface from within us? What do the tragedies we all walk through bring to the surface?

FINDING WORDS

Waking up and following the clues is a good step, but only if it leads to what is really needed here—something so simple, so common, so ordinary, yet something so powerful: words. Even if the word *cancer* is pronounced by the doctor, at least we are no longer faced with a nameless enemy. The truth is out in the open, and we know what we are up against. That's the feel for what's ahead. We have to find words, some spoken expression that forces the voiceless terror out of hiding, the camouflaged lie out into the open.

I'll never forget the first time this happened to me. I had been spiraling down, drowning in depression after my failed attempt as a church planter. I knew I needed help. So I called a longtime friend from college days who had become a counselor. Our weekly phone conversations began to help unwrap the murky layers of my confusion. He would ask perceptive questions and listen, offering feedback along the way. But then he did something else. He asked me to write out some of the painful experiences from my past, forcing me to turn and face those things from which he knew I had been running all these years. So I began to journal those difficult moments, some of which I have already recounted, pulling them up, allowing them to wash over me again. It felt awful, like exhuming a rotting corpse.

And without any warning, it happened. It just popped out on paper, the lie that had driven me for so many years: *It's all my fault.* I remember underlining it and drawing a box around it for emphasis. I had hit the mother lode, from which so many other lies were connected. During those adolescent years, I had unconsciously swallowed the idea that whatever happened was always my fault; that somehow I was to blame for any sense of abandonment, disconnection, and sadness I felt. But now, seeing it in words, out in the open for the first time, I knew it couldn't be true. Sure, I could own my share of the mistakes and sins, but there had been many other

---

It just popped out on paper, the lie that had driven me for so many years: *It's all my fault.*

things I couldn't control, so much that should have happened that didn't. I didn't know the cure yet, but I had found the words, a huge step forward.

This type of experience has happened to me over and over again since that time. One early morning, I was driving to school to begin a routine day of high school teaching. But instead of my usual thoughts focused on all I needed to do before classes began, I stopped to listen to something else. It was a feeling of pressure on my chest, along with a muffled anxiety in my stomach. The nervous energy that came out of this feeling had always made me frustrated with red lights and traffic on the drive in. I had always assumed this was just the normal irritations of the commute and blew it off as that. But this time, I stopped and asked myself, *What is this? Why am I anxious on the way to school each day? Why this pressure over doing something I have done repeatedly for years?* The answer that suddenly came up surprised me: *You still believe you are on trial, onstage, looking for your students' applause, afraid you may come up short, afraid you may be seen as a failure.* It's so obvious to me now, but I had been blind to it for so long. I saw how I had come to school each day with some level of apprehension, triggering a flurry of activity before the first bell, preparation not so much with the students in mind but to make sure that I looked good as a teacher. The energy behind my frantic pace was born of fear, not confidence in the Lord's presence and help. It was anxiety, based on the old promise never to fail in front of others. I could see it now for what it truly was.

It's important to note that what was surfacing in these stories were two types of cancer, two forms of hidden evil. One was the vow we make with all painful or shaming events, never to do something or to allow something to happen again. It is these unspoken commitments lodged deep in our hearts that seem impervious to any form of change. We may commit ourselves to follow Jesus with our minds and even feel passionate in our hearts at times, but the vows remain, binding us, tethering us, keeping us divided. And then there is a deeper cancer, one that lies beneath the vow, one that is often more difficult to find words for. It is a settled conviction about ourselves that tints the way we view everything and everyone around us. It is our corrupted sense of identity, one based on half-truths or outright lies.

One of my friends grew up in a one-parent home with a mother who lived in her own world of constant frenzy and distraction. Feeling the weight of being abandoned emotionally, he was terrified to be alone as a boy. At night in his bedroom, he would turn on the radio just to hear human voices. Somehow the connection seemed to calm him. He would also go to sleep with news magazines strewn all over his bed. If he awoke in the night, the terror of being alone was lessened by seeing pictures of others and being able to read about them. Deep inside of him, a lie was planted at that time, coloring everything he did and said for years: *I am abandoned. No one is ever going to come for me.* That became his core conviction, seemingly truer than anything else he would ever come to believe about God or His Word. What gave the lie such power is that it had enough truth to it to make it convincing. What young boy in that situation wouldn't believe that to be true? But the deception drove him into a life of chasing the parties and the women in college, and then to chasing affirmation as a pastor—all of it with the hope of finding a connection that would always be there for him. But it never worked. The chasing gave the lie more power, only reinforcing his fear of abandonment. Without putting words to the vows and the lies, we, too, become trapped in an increasingly restrictive worldview stemming from our wounded hearts, one that binds us in fear.

In William Golding's gripping novel *Lord of the Flies*, a group of boys are stranded on a deserted island and have to find some way to survive after they realize that rescue isn't coming. The veneer of civilized behavior slowly gets stripped off as they begin to take sides, steal, torture animals, and finally kill each other. But out in the jungle at night, they imagine they have seen a nameless, faceless beast, and it begins to terrorize them. It could come and kill unsuspecting boys. It becomes their worst nightmare. And abiding in the shadows of their minds, without name or form, it remains a terror, finally inciting them to do the unthinkable, mobbing and beating another boy to death with their bare hands. What they couldn't name or see eventually drove them to savagery.

This is a sobering parallel. What we don't know, don't see, and can't name can drive us to do the unthinkable. At the very least, it keeps us divided and trapped. The lie retains its power by staying unknown and unnamed. But to pull it up and expose it is to defang it. The beast can no longer bite; it can no longer tear.

SURFACING AS EXPOSING

This notion of surfacing is woven into the fabric of the New Testament message. So many of Jesus' interactions were cunning maneuvers to surface the lies and expose them with His words. When the prostitute wept on Jesus' feet and washed them with her hair, it was in stark contrast to the cold shoulder He had just received from his dinner host, Simon (Luke 7:36–50). When Simon began to grumble to himself about such outrageous behavior in his own home, Jesus chose not to defend the prostitute or Himself. He simply told a parable, one about forgiveness, with this telling punch line: *he who owes the most debt will love the most when that debt is forgiven*. The point of the parable was to expose the lie Simon had lived under, that somehow his own punctilious concern with the law was going to get him in good standing with God. Jesus came to expose what was hidden from Simon's view, that God doesn't desire dutiful law-abiders. He desires passionate lovers, who relish His forgiveness and delight in His presence. The parable was a shrewd tactic to expose the lies on which Simon had built his entire religious system, lies that were deceiving him and destroying those around him.

Another type of exposure happened when Jesus conversed with Peter after the resurrection (John 21). Jesus had just fixed breakfast for the disciples on the lakeshore after their long night of fishing. Shamed over his public betrayal of Jesus, Peter dreaded the moment when Jesus would surely call him over to condemn him or perhaps publicly renounce him before the other disciples. But underneath the shame was a lie that had settled somewhere deep inside Peter: *My life is over. In His moment of greatest need, I failed my leader and beloved friend. Now I'm useless. I'm no good for anything except to return to my old life of fishing.* After breakfast, Jesus, in fact, did call Peter to Him. The dreaded moment had arrived. Peter braced himself, but what happened next took him completely by surprise. Jesus quietly asked him three times, "Do you love Me?" Each time, Peter quietly responded, "Yes. Lord, You know that I love You." But with the third time, Peter realized this to be Jesus' way of recognizing the betrayal, and now Jesus' responses to Peter probably stunned him: "Take care of My lambs. . . . Shepherd My sheep. . . . Look after My sheep" (vv. 15–17). It's as if Jesus were saying, *Peter, your life isn't over. It's just begun. You think your failure means the end. But it doesn't. It has prepared you to begin. You are not a failure. Your betrayal and shame don't define you before Me. You are My disciple and now My messenger. Go and do something great in My name. Go and shepherd those who will believe in Me. Feed them the truth, and care for them as I have cared for you.*

Jesus surfaced the cancer, exposing the betrayal in a tender and yet unmistakable way. And in refusing to condemn it, He freed Peter from a life of continuous, self-inflicted shame. But He also did something else for Peter: He gave him a mission in life, something that would redefine him and give him his true identity, his place in the great tale that Jesus was authoring. In so doing, He was making Peter into a whole man, an undivided man, a man who could believe with his whole heart and live out of it.

The exposure theme continues throughout the rest of the New Testament. John tells us that we can't continue to walk in the darkness with the light of God shining now in our hearts. To stay in the light, we need to confess our sins, exposing them and bringing them out before ourselves, others, and the Lord (1 John 1:5–9). Paul encouraged all believers to live as children of the light, "because, although you were once the personification of darkness, you are now light in the Lord" (Eph. 5:8). And later on in the passage he adds this: "Everything exposed by the light becomes visible, for it is light that makes everything visible" (vv. 13–14 NIV). This is not stating the obvious concerning the physics of light. Paul was implying that what gives the darkness its power is the darkness itself. It is the hiding, the burying, the concealing that makes evil seem so formidable. But once the light of truth hits it, it shrinks and flees because it's all visible now. Think of the Great and Terrible Oz frightening Dorothy and her companions with his booming voice and theatrical props in *The Wizard of Oz*. Then think of Toto pulling the curtain aside to expose an old and weak man. That's the feel of exposing here.

_____

You can surface and expose everything now, not to be shamed by it but to be transformed out of it.

But the exposure theme widens still further when we realize that everything is one day going to be exposed. In fact, the New Testament speaks about judgment in just such terms, as a time when nothing is going to be hidden anymore: "This good news given to me declares that this *affirmation and accusation* will take place on that day when God, through Jesus, the Anointed One, judges every person's life secrets" (Rom. 2:16). On that day, there will be no more secrets, no more whisperings in the dark, no more attempts to keep something out of sight. Some of us may respond to a statement like this with fear and trepidation. That only goes to show how much we still live in hiding. The wonder of the New Testament message is that no one has to wait for that kind of forced stripping, when all will be laid bare. You can surface and expose everything now, not to be shamed by it but to be transformed out of it.

But even if these truths aren't compelling enough, there is a final reason to submit to exposure. Living in darkness is wearying. Hiding from everyone is exhausting. I have repeatedly heard men and women speak of the expansive freedom they experience when their own darkness finally gets exposed. Just recently I heard the story of a well-known reporter who became an alcoholic to deal with her panic attacks, ones that stemmed from her father's constant absence during childhood. She spoke about the initial shame of it all when the story became public, but that soon gave way to something she had never known: freedom. For the first time ever, she was free from the burden of having to hide it all for another day. Perhaps surfacing isn't so unappealing or harsh after all. Maybe it's what we long for. To drop the terrible weight of the false self is our first significant motion

---

Living in darkness is wearying. Hiding from everyone is exhausting.

toward becoming undivided men and women. We will need this encouragement, for the journey ahead to surface and expose is strewn with danger. It will sometimes take a courage we didn't know we possessed just to continue. Just ask Truman.

The Truman Show is the unconventional tale of Truman Burbank, a man who thinks he lives a normal life with a normal job in a normal house with a normal wife. But his life is anything but normal. He is in fact the star of a reality TV show about his life that has been airing worldwide since the day he was conceived. As the movie goes on, he gets more and more clues that something is wrong with his life, that the way it is presented to him may actually be a front, even a lie. For everyone in Truman's life, even his wife, knows the truth about Truman. The only person who doesn't is Truman himself. But to discover the truth, he has to keep following the clues, leading him to face his deepest terror, the open water of the ocean. In the end, Truman chooses to face the terror and sail into the ocean, where he finally discovers the truth about his life. But he not only finds the truth here—he finds himself, his true identity. He becomes his namesake: a *true man.*

So many of the great stories contain this same germ of truth. There is a deep lie in us and around us, an insidious cancer that is largely unknown and unnoticed. And the task before us is to surface the lie so that we can embrace the truth and discover our truest identity. By taking such a journey, we will discover, to our surprise, the gap starting to close between our heads and hearts. But this is only the start of tackling the divide. We have to do something with the lies we have now surfaced. We have to hear the truth. We have to learn to listen.

PRAYER:

Father, I am riddled with lies. Just because I believe Your truth in my head, it doesn't mean that I believe it with my heart. There are so many places in my heart that feel bound and gagged. I have been deceived about You and about myself in so many ways. The lies have been cruel taskmasters. What makes them even crueler is that I don't know what they are. Teach me to be attentive to my heart and to be attentive to You. Every day I know You are trying to get my attention, trying to get me to understand. You want to set me free. I want to be set free. Expose the lies so that I can hear the truth, so that I can hear You. I ache for the truth. I ache for You.

FATHER: *My child, you are right. There is much work to be done in your heart. There is much that is holding you back. And I have been seeking after you for a long time. Turn and ask Me about the thoughts and feelings you have each day. I will help expose the lies. Through My Son, I am your true Father. Let Me be a Father to you. Let me guide you. Let me set you free.*

QUESTIONS FOR JOURNALING AND DISCUSSION

1. Pick a quote from this chapter that you found especially helpful or insightful. Describe what you got out of it.

2. The lies inside us can surface when we become attentive to our hearts. This can occur in so many places:
   - in our response to a story
   - in the daily frustrations of life
   - in our inner dialogue
   - during times of conflict
   - while walking through tragedy

   Pick one or two of these to think through more deeply. Describe what happened and your response. What were you feeling? What were you thinking? Do you know why you responded that way?

3. Make a list of the lies in your heart that you are aware of. Which ones are more like vows? Which ones are more like statements about your identity?

4. Read again how Jesus surfaced the cancer in Peter's heart in John 21:1–17. Does the idea of Jesus surfacing the cancer in your heart scare you? Confuse you? Excite you? Why?

5. Respond to the idea of future judgment as exposing everything, when all secrets will be laid bare. What questions does this arouse? What fears? What hopes?

LISTENING

None so deaf as those that will not hear.

—Matthew Henry [1]

It was supposed to be an ordinary conversation with my father, but the ordinary soon turned into something else. My father now lives in a retirement home, and on my visits to him, I try to catch him up on recent events and hear how he is doing. But as the conversation progressed on this visit, I kept having to repeat words. He was misunderstanding final consonants, where *bread* became *breath* and *shock* became *shot*. He would then miss whole words, asking me to repeat a sentence. I turned up the volume of my voice a notch in an effort to clarify. It helped somewhat, but the need to reiterate continued, along with a growing irritation inside of me. I was over-enunciating and over-projecting, way out of line for a quiet conversation in his living room. In the back of my mind, I was wondering, *What is wrong with my father? Why can't he just focus and listen?* Suddenly, my father sprang off the sofa with these four words: "The batteries are dead." And with that he left the room.

I knew immediately what had happened. As long as I have known my father, he has worn hearing aids. His loss of hearing began with a prolonged ear infection as a boy, before the age of antibiotics.

With military duty during World War II and the sound of guns and artillery, the deafness only deepened. Yet when his hearing aids are working properly, I hardly notice his problem. I even forget he wears them. That's why I was so irritated and then puzzled with our conversation. I'm so used to speaking to him in a normal tone of voice.

I have known others with the same issue. My good friend Bruce has to wear hearing aids because of duck hunting without proper ear protection during his younger years. Dede is another friend who has to wear them because of calcium buildup on her ear bones, a condition diagnosed during her high school years. They both deal with their impairment with a level of grace and humor, but others have struggled with it deeply. I knew one young man whose hearing loss affected both his understanding and his speech, yet he would sometimes refuse to wear his hearing aids, probably out of shame. The shame factor is especially prominent in the story of Derrick Coleman, the first-ever NFL offensive player to be legally deaf. He has become an inspiration to many who suffer with the same difficulty, but his triumph didn't start that way. He became deaf at an early age due to a genetic anomaly. His oversized hearing aids in elementary school became a target for cruel taunts from other kids. Yet his relentless drive and athletic ability kept him persevering until he found himself on the winning team of the Super Bowl.[2]

But the whole struggle to hear isn't just something that those who are truly hearing impaired deal with. I got this reminder daily during my years in the high school classroom. To give just one

---

**It's a universal blight.
We are all deaf.
We are all listening impaired.**

example, I remember announcing the homework for the next day in one particular class and pointing it out in written form on the board. A few minutes later, a young man raised his hand and asked, "Mr. Delvaux, do we have any homework?" My response was frustration, mixed with incredulity. How could a student miss something so obvious, given both a visual and a verbal clue? I know exactly how.

It happened recently in a conversation with Heidi as we rehearsed the day's events for each other. She was relating a story, but in the middle of it, she pulled up and suddenly asked, "Bill, you have that blank stare in your eyes. You aren't listening, are you?" She had caught me. I hadn't been listening. Something from our conversation had triggered another thought in my mind, and I was far away, on another planet, with my own problems and pressures, hearing the reverberations of her words pass through my eardrums, but not registering a word she was saying. If this were just a momentary glitch, it would be understandable. But it's not. My tendency to drift back into my private world isn't just irritating to Heidi. It has hurt her as well. It feels like a repeat performance of her own father, who also didn't know how to listen or be attentive to her. But the whole struggle to listen suddenly takes on epic proportions when I peer beyond my own world. As I have watched and interacted with parents and teenagers, husbands and wives, I've learned that the inability to listen isn't just taxing or vexing. It decimates. How many families and marriages have I seen shredded for one simple reason: the inability to listen. It seems that this handicap doesn't just affect those with hearing aids. It's a universal blight. We are all deaf. We are all listening impaired.

THE JOURNEY AHEAD

Remember where we are on this journey of tackling the divide between our heads and hearts. In a fallen world largely cut off from the glory and wonder of God, with a fallen self similarly cut off from connection to God, among other fallen souls in the same plight, we become fertile ground for a toxic growth of lies and vows, a cancer that germinates in us at some point and begins to flourish. The shame often intertwined with this malignancy insists that we push it all down and keep it concealed. The result is the normal fallen humanity we see every day, each of us fractured into the person we project and the person we bury, torn between ideas we hold to be true and the feelings we can't control. The divide doesn't necessarily mend when we come to Jesus. In fact, it can feel more pressing. We are now new creations in Christ, and the truths of the Bible are supposed to set us free. Yet the divide rears its head at some point and defiantly challenges us: *With all this new knowledge, why aren't you changing?* And with that question, we start to question our-selves: *Why am I not getting better? Why am I still wrestling with anger at my spouse? Why does work still consume me? Why am I so anxious about my future? Why does God seem so far away? Why do I still feel like a little child at times? Why am I so afraid of what others think of me?* And with these unsettling questions come the darker doubts: *Something's wrong with me. Maybe this works for others, but not for me. Maybe I'm not good enough for God. Maybe He loves others, but not me. Perhaps nothing will ever change. Maybe I'm just doomed.* Without others voicing these same struggles, we cower and hide ourselves further from view, afraid that we are alone, dividing ourselves still deeper.

Forward momentum requires something else: We have to tackle the divide. We have to face the tyrant that has defied us. We have to stare down the terror that has mocked us. This has meant surfacing the cancer and finding words for it. But diagnosis isn't enough. Without hope for improvement, diagnosis can be despair. What we need is a cure. And the cure here isn't a new concept we grab hold of or a new task we take on. It's something much more ordinary and unexceptional, something we do every day. It's listening.

It is nearly impossible to exaggerate the importance of listening. What we hear or don't hear from a teacher may be the difference between failing and passing. What we hear or don't hear from a friend may be the difference between betrayal and loyalty. What we hear or don't hear from a child may be the difference between shame and encouragement. What we hear or don't hear from a spouse may be the difference between conflict and compassion. But let's flip it around. We all know what it feels like to be the one who is heard. We feel important, understood, known, and loved. One of my acquaintances is an author and counselor, a man I see only twice a year. Yet every time we meet for morning coffee, I look forward to it more than so many of my other meetings. As I was driving away from one of our recent conversations, it suddenly struck me why I enjoy our times together. He listens so attentively. I feel so understood.

But the importance of listening doesn't stop here with others. There is one more level to ascend. What we hear or don't hear from God can be the difference between life and death. One of the last things Moses said to the Israelites emphasizes this clearly: "Every word I've said to you today *will be a witness against you*, so set it in

---

The divide doesn't necessarily mend when we come to Jesus. In fact, it can feel more pressing.

your heart, *remember it well.* . . . You can't afford to ignore even one word; your very life depends on it!" (Deut. 32:46–47). To listen attentively, to take to heart the words of God—that means life. To refuse means death. Just a casual scan of Old Testament history shows how true this turned out to be. But the same pattern arises in the New Testament. To hear the words of Jesus and follow Him is the path to life. To refuse to listen is death. Yet to hear and follow Him is not just a onetime occurrence. Walking with Him, staying connected to Him, requires that we continue to listen and take to heart all He is trying to say. But therein lies the rub. We're so hearing impaired.

WHY WE ARE DEAF

Why the deafness, the inability to attune to truth, to take it to heart? The most obvious obstacle may be the incessant sound of our own busyness. A school administrator once admitted to me he had nine thousand e-mails in his in-box. Here was a man who consistently and diligently tried to keep up with the pace of work thrown at him—yet this is where it landed him. Repeatedly I have heard this story in the workplace, how technology has upped the standards on production, how employers are asked to do more with less, how a quicker response is expected to emails and phone calls even on nights and weekends, how boundaries have become blurred between career and home. One friend on a backpacking trip with me once confided that it took him forty-eight hours to detox from the rush of the workplace. It took him that long in the wilderness to drop everything and leave it behind. Only then could he really learn to be still and listen.

But the frenetic pace of life also spreads from the office into the home. Once I asked a group of high school students how many of them ate dinner with their families. I was shocked at how few of them did with any regularity. And these were, in general, good students from stable homes. It seems that sitting for a meal, recapping the day, and listening to each other has become a family relic of the past. We are too busy for such luxuries.

But there are other obstacles besides the normative rush of life. Our entrenched patterns of unbelief, creating tangled commitments to idols, wrap a blanket of fog around us, blocking connection with God and plugging our ears from the truth. Several years ago, I went backpacking with my friend Rodney in the Roan Mountain area in East Tennessee. Here the Appalachian Trail rides atop a chain of bald mountains, producing a sweeping panorama that makes this one of the most popular sections of the entire trail. Camping one night in a gap between two of the balds gave us an opportunity to breathe in the expansive vistas. But the next morning before packing up, we saw an ominous cloudbank moving swiftly toward us. Knowing the temperamental character of mountain weather, we looked at each other with some concern, threw our gear into the packs, and headed out quickly to descend. But the cloudbank was faster. Racing toward us, it caught us near the top of the next bald. What had been a sweeping panorama instantly became a white prison. We were locked inside a fog bank so thick that visibility dropped to five yards. We had no idea what was around us or what was ahead of us. It was unnerving to feel so cut off, and without a clearly marked path in the grass, it could have been a disaster.

Our self-chosen idols function in the same way. They become a cloudbank overrunning our hearts, cutting us off from connection to the living God and attenuating our spiritual hearing. We run to them, searching for the water of life, hoping to find something to ease our inward thirst; instead, they imprison us. One friend recently admitted how his idol of comfort has kept his heart disengaged from others and from God. Looking for the easy way out always meant steering clear of relational unknowns and potential conflicts, even though he was desperately needed as a husband and father. But the real tragedy of such disengagement is that it has cut off his sense of communion with God. It has fogged over that connection so that he can't feel much of anything now, even though he craves it. My own idol of approval and affirmation kept me for years on a spinning wheel of performing and demanding. I not only manipulated others, but I also became deaf to the approval God wanted to give me. Even though I knew He loved me beyond all human understanding, I had no feel for it, no sense of living in it or out of it for the sake of others. In the end, whatever we run to instead of God keeps us deaf, unable to hear His truth.

There are also other voices that relentlessly call out to us, that override the voice of truth. They are the voices of our wounding, the places where our hearts have been impaled. They call out to us in strident tones, ceaselessly reminding us of what appears to be the truth about life. With such relentless voices coercing us, how can we possibly hear any other voice? How is a woman to hear and receive the Father's love and delight when the only men she has known reduced her to a sexual toy, abusing her and degrading her? How is a man to understand and listen to the Father's approval when he grew up on a continual diet of criticism and manipulation from his own father? How is a boy supposed to know his unique and unutterably special place in the heart of God when his classmates have taunted and bullied him? How is a girl supposed to take in the love of Jesus for her heart when she has been told, both verbally and nonverbally,

In the end, whatever we run to instead of God keeps us deaf, unable to hear His truth.

that she is ugly and unwanted by boys of social power and standing? How is a young man supposed to believe in the strength that God wants to give him when the coach has shamed him for his weakness and failure in front of the team? How can anyone hear truth when these types of wounds are inflicted? I wish these stories were hypothetical. They aren't. The wounds fester and weep, and their voices cry out to us day and night.

I experienced a telling parallel to these relentless voices when I had the opportunity to visit the Marine Corps boot camp. Educators are regularly invited in to get an up-close view of the program. It's a good marketing ploy for the Marines, and it works. Seeing a new cadre of Marines graduating from the boot camp was impressive and inspirational. But there were other moments that were unnerving. We were allowed to get a taste of the notorious drill sergeants at work when they were unleashed on our group of educators for a brief stint. All in good fun, but it was still unsettling to hear someone yell at you incessantly, whether you obeyed the orders or not. I was glad when this short demonstration was over, but it doesn't end for those in the real boot camp. The screaming never stops. The pressure never lets up. Our core wounds function just like these drill sergeants, yelling at us, insisting that we listen to them and obey. No other option seems possible. How then can we possibly listen to God?

However, there is another equally difficult obstacle, one that runs entirely in the other direction. It's not the sound of voices yelling at us; it's the sound of silence. We are often awkward with it, even fearful of it. Heidi and I have noticed this in worship services we have attended over the years. Times for quiet prayer are barely long enough to collect your thoughts, much less pray, and even that supposed moment of quiet often has music vamped underneath. The idea of being still, of silencing the phone, of shutting down the computer, of turning off the music, of removing ourselves from the swirl of activity engenders a vague uneasiness, for all of the noise has been keeping something at bay. In our refusal to be silent, we have been unconsciously running from something, hoping it won't catch us. Our whole sense of being has become tethered to the next business deal, the next phone call, the next Facebook post, the next party or workout or night out. All the motion here is not a motion forward. We are retreating, afraid of stopping, of what may happen, of what we may meet. The irony is that our attempt to outrun this unnamed pursuer is doomed from the start. It can never be outrun. We will be tracked down at some point and caught. Why? Because the pursuer is us. We have been running from ourselves.

A friend once told the story of his own attempt to run. He spent years using his music, his wife, and his ministry as a surrogate mother. Everything and everyone became something to be manipulated to meet the throbbing ache for comfort and love. He couldn't be by himself. He couldn't be silent. His terror was one of facing his own existential aloneness, of having all apron strings cut, of having to stand naked and unsupported. We think such aloneness will kill us. What we don't realize is that it will save us. In the naked silence, God will meet us.

I once took a group of fathers and sons to a ropes course for a morning of adventure and challenge. One of the activities was an obstacle course about thirty yards long, set among some trees and underbrush. There were metal objects hanging by ropes from the branches above, plus tires, wood, and rocks strewn all over the course. Each son was sent to the start of the course and then blindfolded. The dads were placed at the end of it and told they could guide their sons with their voices in any way that would help. Only one problem: there were five fathers, all yelling at the same time. The son had to focus on his father's voice and tune out all the others. Even then, the sons found themselves tripping, banging their heads, and losing their way. This is as good a parallel as I know. How are we to hear the voice of truth, the voice of the Father, when there are so many other voices screaming at us, when the obstacles are everywhere? How are we to overcome our hearing impairment?

LISTENING AS OBEYING

But our predicament only deepens when the idea of hearing is explored in the Bible. To hear, to listen, to take to heart all that God is saying means something more than just hearing the sound and receiving the truth. To hear is to obey. One of the most well-known verses in the Old Testament begins with a call to hear: "Hear, O Israel, the LORD our God, the LORD is one. Love the LORD your God with all your heart and with your soul and with all your strength" (Deut. 6:4–5 NIV). To hear that the Lord is the one God is to ruthlessly strip away any idol, any structure, any habit that entangles our hearts, and then offer our love to God alone, with everything that we are and hope to be. It seems that the listening required here reaches inside, down into our deepest substructures, and then reorients them so that we follow a new path outwardly. Only this type of hearing will connect us to God. Only this type of hearing will save us from ourselves.

The New Testament picks up this same link between listening and obeying. At the end of Jesus' stunning hillside sermon, He appended a postscript in the form of a parable (Matt. 7:24–27). If we hear His words and put them into practice, we are like the man who built his house on a rock, one that will withstand all the coming storms. But if we hear His words and do nothing with them, we are constructing our homes on shifting sand that will one day wash away.

We find here the two tales of the Bible once more, this time delineated by one's obedience.

The book of James picks up this same idea with an apt analogy: listening to the words of God and doing nothing with them is like looking casually at oneself in the mirror, then turning away and immediately forgetting one's own likeness. James continues with this striking comment: "However, it is possible to open your eyes and take in the beautiful, perfect truth found in God's law of liberty *and live by it*. If you pursue that path and actually do what God has commanded, then you will avoid *the many distractions that lead to* an amnesia of all true things and you will be blessed" (James 1:25). It is open eyes along with attentive ears that yield a life of following and doing. Somehow the listening that Jesus asks of all His followers is a type of listening that stains us like wood stain. It can't peel off like paint because it has permanently soaked down in us and through us, altering the very tone and texture of our hearts and then radically altering our outward lives.

But again, there's the rub. How do we learn to do this? How do we gaze intently and listen attentively this way? We learn by thinking carefully about those moments when we already are listening attentively. We all do it at some point, and those attentive moments often come on us by surprise. One of them happened to me this way.

LEARNING FROM A STRANGE SOURCE

A number of years ago, I was reading a novel by Scottish author George MacDonald titled *Robert Falconer*. The story opens with a young boy being raised by a religiously strict and fearful grandmother. All he knows of his father is that his dad has done something bad and run off, leaving the boy fatherless. The grandmother's silence on the matter seems deafening to him, and he longs to go and find his father. One night the son has a remarkable dream sequence in which the wall behind his bed opens out onto the Scottish landscape of heather and stone, where he sees men passing by, men whom he knows are his ancestors. Four of them suddenly appear in the room with him, and from the little he knows of his family history, he recognizes the first three to be his father, grandfather, and great-grandfather, dressed in the clothes they would have worn for that time. But the boy's wonder widens when his great-great-grandfather appears in Highlander clothing with a broadsword at his side. The boy awakes, perplexed by the dream, and soon forgets it as he comes down to breakfast that morning.

But my response was anything but forgetfulness. When I began to read the dream sequence, something unknown stirred inside me. My heart opened in growing wonder and then surprise as the dream continued. I read it again several times and marked it. Something important was being said. Was I listening? As I thought about it, I suddenly understood. At that point in my journey as a man, I had become aware of a generational void I had been raised in. My father had said almost nothing about his father and absolutely nothing about his grandfather. For me, they were names in a genealogy chart, pictures on a wall, nothing more. But over time, I intuited the void to mean something. I was missing a piece I needed to recover to continue the journey. But as is the case in so many of these situations, I didn't know what I didn't know.

Somehow the listening that Jesus asks of all His followers is a type of listening that stains us like wood stain.

It was the dream sequence that revealed to me what I didn't know, the next place I needed to head. I had already done much work in restoring the strained relationship with my father. Our conversations had unearthed many unaddressed topics of the past, things unspoken about his family, remembrances as a boy, and his own hopes for and sadness about our family. But I needed to ask him more about his father and grandfather, both of whom I never knew. I started to ply him with questions and then one day made a huge discovery. My grandfather was unable to get beyond the eighth grade due to sickness in the family. He had to stop his education and go to work. To overcome this, he became a voracious reader, delving into literature an hour or two every night. I, too, had a thirst for books and reading, and realized that I had perhaps inherited this from him. It wasn't just information anymore to me. It was connection. I felt tied to him. For years I had hated my father and, in so doing, had hated my ancestry. But that had only led to hating myself. As I turned back toward my father and my ancestry, I found them to be fallen and fallible, like me, and yet real, touchable, approachable. In that turning back, I didn't just find genealogical tidbits. I found part of myself.

I tell this story because it is the pattern of listening we are called to. What is ironic is that at that point I was listening to George MacDonald much better than I sometimes listen to God's Word. And the listening took me through different stages, each with its own motion and function. First I was attentive. Whenever I read MacDonald, I always find myself hungry, open to receiving something from his writings. Everything else gets blocked out. I am focused, locked in. Then came understanding. When the dream sequence occurred in the story, I read it through several times until I under-stood in sharper detail the actual events of the dream. Then came the revelation, that what I was missing in my life was right there, that something about my own lineage was being pointed out. And finally, the revelation led to doing something, to initiating conversations with my father that became so nourishing and healing. This is the type of attentive gaze we need. This is how we become stained with truth and how the head and heart start to converge. We are listening.

HUNGRY LISTENING

Once we come to Christ, we are called to this type of listening, a hungry listening, one with the heart awake and longing, ready to hear, ready to respond. The book of Isaiah gives a striking image of this kind of listening. In one section describing the coming Messiah, Isaiah painted an intimate portrait of listening to God: "The Sovereign LORD has given me an instructed tongue to know the word that sustains the weary. He wakens me morning by morning, wakens my ear to listen like one being taught. The Sovereign LORD has opened my ears, and I have not been rebellious; I have not drawn back" (50:4–5 NIV). If the coming King of all glory, if Jesus Himself, needed to listen and be instructed by His Father each morning so that He could uplift the weary and downcast, how much more His followers need to listen! Imagine being greeted each morning by the sounds of the sunrise, the stirrings of the new day, and the whispers of the heavenly Father. You sense His mouth close to your ear. You feel the warmth of His presence. You are aware of the strength of His attentiveness. Your heart knows the tasks at hand for the day. You can already see the obstacles and challenges ahead. You are hungry, open, ready to receive, ready to obey. You are listening.

Jesus Himself intimated that His true followers are to listen to Him in this same way, in the close, intimate way He listens to the Father. In some of the parables addressed to the crowds, He ended with this cryptic comment: "He who has ears to hear, let him hear" (Matt. 13:9). Only those in the throng who listened with hungry hearts would be able to hear, receive, and act on the subtle messages of the parables. They alone would be His true followers.

With His own band of twelve disciples, we find this same attentive listening required. As He faced His impending torture and death, Jesus asked them to remain with Him, to bond to Him, as He did with His own Father. How were they to do that? One clue comes in John 15:7: "If you abide in Me and My voice abides in you, anything you ask will come to pass for you." He seemed to equate their abiding in Him with His voice remaining in them. To listen to that voice and retain His truth would keep them bonded to him. It would also give them immense latitude and confidence as they prayed. He was asking His disciples to be hungry listeners. This is how they were to follow Him and become like Him. This is how they would pray in the kingdom, overcome the odds, and attempt the impossible. It was to be their pathway into that second tale of redemption. It's our path also.

What does it look like to listen this way to the truth of the Bible? It means coming to the Scriptures with the cancer exposed, hungry for the cure. It means hearing the truth with longing hearts, alert to Jesus' words. Here is one example that happened to me recently. As I have moved out of the familiar harbor of the classroom and into the choppy waters of writing and speaking, the fear of failure has continued to haunt me and sometimes engulf me. To keep navigating

His kingdom is the one venture that cannot fail, the one enterprise that cannot be thwarted, the one endeavor that cannot be stopped.

forward, I have had to trust and let go of so many security props. With this fear very much present one morning, I was reading the story of the angel's announcement of the virgin birth to Mary. She was left breathless, confused, and stunned. How could she bear a child without ever having intimately known a man? The angel replied that it would be the work of the Holy Spirit and finished with this telling statement: "No word from God will ever fail" (Luke 1:37 NIV). The same experience happened here parallel to my reading of MacDonald. I was aching, hungry, hoping to receive that morning. After I read the passage, I let it soak in, writing down the verse, journaling about it, trying to understand it, letting it filter into me.

But then the revelation came; the magic happened. The truth suddenly arced back to my hunger. I saw something I had never seen before. This is what I wrote in my journal: "This is how the impossible happens. It's not me—it's the Father doing His work. I want to do what you are doing. For you never fail in what you do." Then I wrote this: "wow—this is huge. All of my fear of failure is about me looking successful. But what if I bond to my Father and what he is doing? He never fails." And the revelation led me to action, to letting go of attempts to look successful that day and asking the Father to teach me to do His work. It was a deep liberation for me and continues to be. For His kingdom is the one venture that cannot fail, the one enterprise that cannot be thwarted, the one endeavor that cannot be stopped. To become a tagalong on this undertaking changes everything. This is not about me or anybody else. This is about His kingdom, one that can never fail.

My ability to listen to the Bible each day is not always as momentous, but there are often quieter encounters that leave me stained with the truth I need to hear for that day. I still struggle with the fear of failure, but much less so. And when I do, I seek to recall the truth.

The vow I made in the seventh grade with that basketball game is slowly being broken. I am learning to listen.

PRAYER:

Father, I admit that I am deaf. I listen to everything else. I know so little of what it means to listen to You. The tangled web of lies and idols, the fear of aloneness and silence, and the incessant noise of the world—it all drowns out Your truth and Your voice. I come to You lost and afraid. I want to listen. I want to hear You with my heart. And I want to love You and obey You, but my heart is so tied and trained to obeying all the other voices. I don't even know where to start, except to say that I want to hear You, really hear You. I want your truth to stain me and color me. I want it to replace the lies that have seduced me and imprisoned me. Come and rescue me. Teach me to be a child again, a child who listens to the voice of his Father.

FATHER: *My child, to admit that you are deaf is the first step in listening. Yes, there is a long road ahead to untangle the knots and cut the bonds that have imprisoned you. But you are not left alone to do this. I gave My Son for you. I will also surely come and give you the counsel you need to follow Him. Remember, I long for you to listen also, for I long for your company, for your heart, for you.*

QUESTIONS FOR JOURNALING AND DISCUSSION

1. Pick one quote that you found to be especially helpful or insightful. Describe what you got out of it.

2. Take some of the inner questions and doubts posed in the section "The Journey Ahead." The list starts with *Why am I not getting better?* Which ones do you identify with? What are some other questions or doubts you have about the change needed in your life?

3. Listed below are the obstacles to hearing God's truth delineated in this chapter:
   - incessant busyness of life
   - fog created by our idols
   - voices of our wounds
   - fear of aloneness and silence

   Take one or two that you are most aware of right now and describe how they function in your life. How exactly do they keep you from listening?

4. Is there a story or an analogy from this chapter that especially struck you as you read it? What do you think is behind your reaction?

5. Look again at the link between listening and obeying in Matthew 7:24–27 and James 1:22–25. What do you see in this link that you find disturbing or challenging? What do you find comforting or hopeful?

6. "Imagine being greeted each morning by the sounds of the sunrise, the stirrings of the new day, and the whispers of the

heavenly Father. You sense His mouth close to your ear. You feel the warmth of His presence. You are aware of the strength of His attentiveness. Your heart knows the tasks at hand for the day. You can already see the obstacles and challenges ahead. You are hungry, open, ready to receive, ready to obey. You are listening." This is a description of hungry listening. What does it stir inside of you?

TELLING

> Why, then, do I set before You an ordered account of so many things? It's certainly not through me that You know them. But I'm stirring up love for You in myself and in those who read this so that we may all say, great is the Lord and highly worthy to be praised. I tell my story for love of Your love.
>
> **—Augustine,** *Confessions*[1]

The minister one Sunday morning had been teaching through a passage in the Gospels. Much of it was familiar terrain for the congregation—no startling revelations, just good reminders of the faith. At first, everyone seemed to be focused on what he was saying, but as the sermon progressed, some in the crowd struggled to remain attentive, yawning or becoming distracted with fidgety children. The sound of coughing and the rattling of paper could be heard, interspersed with the minister's voice. But as the sermon drew to a close, something unexpected happened. He suddenly switched from the Bible to his life, recounting a part of his story. He spoke of his calling to be a minister that began during adolescence, yet his fear of rejection and sense of inadequacy had left him in despair over ever attempting to be one. He tried to drown out the calling in college by immersing himself in alcohol and parties only to find God still after him when he graduated. I was in the congregation that morning and found myself sucked into his story, surprised at his raw candor. But then I noticed something else. It wasn't just me. I looked around and saw the same response everywhere. The coughs and yawns had stopped. There was no more shuffling of paper. Even the children had all become still. A tense silence hovered over the entire assembly, eyes locked in on the speaker. For a few minutes, time froze, and we all forgot where we were, what we were doing after the service, or even our own cares and worries. Something remarkable was being offered to us, and we all knew it. To this day, I don't remember anything he said in the sermon. But I'll remember his story forever.

A similar moment happened at another church where Heidi and I were attending. There was an announcement about an upcoming conference on relationships, and a church leader got up to describe the conference's impact on him the previous year. But instead of speaking about it in general terms, he spoke about his own failings as a father and husband and how the conference had helped him come to terms with it. I was startled by his honesty, and so was Heidi. She looked at me and said, "I could go home now." I think I could have also. We had heard something exceptional that morning that had nourished us, something fragile and yet wielding great power. We had heard someone's story.

We had heard something exceptional that morning that had nourished us, something fragile and yet wielding great power. We had heard someone's story.

Tackling the divide between our heads and hearts has led us through some unusual terrain so far. We have hacked our way out from the tangled undergrowth of lies and vows. We then traversed our way through a special type of listening, a hungry listening. Both of these have involved work that we primarily do on our own. But as we approach this final leg of tackling the divide, there is a distinct shift. For healing the divide can never be a sole enterprise. It's our isolation that got us into trouble in the first place. Remember how the chasm opened for Adam and Eve, how their refusal to trust God with the good and grasping for it themselves led them into shame, that violating sense of exposure before another. As a relational violation, shame is something we can't undo by ourselves. We can't discover a self-help therapy for it—one doesn't exist. It can only be cured in the company of others. That's what this third and last section is all about. It's about allowing others to help us close the divide and then helping them as well.

THE COMMUNAL AS PRIORITY

This sort of communal endeavor is tightly woven into the fabric of the entire Bible. God certainly calls us out and deals with us as individuals, yet there is also a high priority on community throughout Scripture. The Old Testament focuses on the nation of Israel as a whole time and time again, not just on individuals in that nation, as it reveals God's thoughts and intentions toward Israel and their response to Him. A similar tone is felt throughout the New Testament, especially noticeable in the commands using the reciprocal pronoun *one another*: honor one another; encourage one another; be devoted to one another; accept one another; be subject to one another; bear with one another; live in peace with one another; serve one another. Then there are the negative injunctions of the same type: do not complain against one another; do not lie to one another; do not judge one another.

This reciprocity of action is not just an interesting addendum in the life of a Christ follower. It's front and center, and it's that way for a reason. Jesus put it there: "A new command I give you: Love one another. As I have loved you, so you must love one another" (John 13:34 NIV). To follow Jesus is to follow with others close by, on our right and left. This is the framework we are given by him.

None of this is meant to contradict the place of the individual, that each heart is precious to God, that Jesus approaches each of us uniquely and beautifully. But the weight of the message given in the Bible involves the communal. It's such an obvious point, but one often overlooked. Unconsciously, especially in the West, we can assume the opposite, that the life of following Jesus is by and large an individualistic effort with others thrown in here and there to help matters when we can't manage anymore on our own. This is another way our own reading of the Bible ends up deepening the divide instead of healing it. I know this so well from my own errors on this point.

Interestingly, modern research on the brain supports the priority of the communal. We now know that there is no such thing as an individual brain, not even an individual neuron; that from the moment of our birth, we are reading the environment, mimicking behavior, body language, and language itself. Without this type of constant connection, the brain can't even exist, much less grow or function.[2] If there is any doubt about this, just ask someone who has been to an orphanage where babies have been neglected or abandoned. It's heart-wrenching to see the emotional damage inflicted on these little ones. But this is exactly the same damage we inflict on ourselves when we try to go it alone. It's just as heart-wrenching. The Bible's call to walk with others as we walk with God isn't something opposed to our fundamental natures. It's written in the very neural circuitry of our brains.

But even more surprising is the research that has been done on telling one's own story and listening to the stories of others. There are actual physical changes in the brain when we feel heard by someone else as we speak, and those changes extend to the brain of the one listening attentively to us. Something happens in the very hard wiring of those complex neural networks.[3] It's what I had felt that Sunday morning when the minister told his story of fear and inadequacy. It's what the whole congregation felt in that charged silence. They weren't just listening to good theology anymore, even profound and enriching theology, as helpful and as needed as that is. They were listening differently. They were listening to a person. They were listening to the heart of a man stripping himself of ministerial pretenses, a man who was fearful and confused, a man very much like themselves. They were connecting to him, and in that moment they were changing.

Two specific reciprocal commands in the Bible touch on this aspect of storytelling. James, the brother of Jesus, pulled no punches here: "Therefore, confess your sins to each other and pray for each other so that you may be healed" (James 5:16 NIV). The very places we instinctively tuck away, the places where the barbs of shame are most keenly felt, these are precisely the places we are to reveal to others. Our confession can prompt their intercession, and that in turn can prompt our healing. Solo confession, though needed, won't

---

The Bible's call to walk with others as we walk with God isn't something opposed to our fundamental natures. It's written in the very neural circuitry of our brains.

do it. We need more. We need others. In a parallel way, we find Paul admonishing his hearers: "Shoulder each other's burdens, and then you will live as the law of the Anointed teaches us" (Gal. 6:2). The burdens of this life, its struggles and pressures, its hardships and grief, cannot be managed or negotiated on our own. We have to share our load with others and then return the favor. This is how we are to keep the law of Christ, the law of love. How exactly are we to bear each other's burdens? That all depends on the exact nature of the burden. But one thing I do know: just in the telling and receiving of the burden, something striking happens, something that lessens the load right in that moment. I know this now from so many encounters. But one of the most striking happened with my own mother.

Mom was the quintessential Southern woman, marked by a cheerful hospitality and a generous spirit. She became a mentor and friend to a great number of other women, many of whom have spoken to me of her influence on their lives. Her warmth and grace were also characteristic of our interactions at home. With a mother like that, what could possibly be wrong? Yet, as I matured into an adult, I felt a troubling disconnect from her, mixed with a brooding, residual anger. Because of her winsome personality, I blamed the problem on myself for years. And without the resolve to confront her about it, I kept it at bay, underground, swirling in a matrix of guilt and avoidance. Part of the problem was that I just didn't know what *it* was. But something crystallized when my mother developed terminal stomach cancer. Suddenly I realized I didn't know a thing about her. Sure, I knew the outline of her story as a child, the basic facts of her education and marriage, and the funny stories she told so well. But about her, about her heart, about her yearnings and disappointments, her hopes and anxieties, I knew almost nothing. It was the void that had been nagging at me all those years.

For my mother, part of being that quintessential Southern woman was being the strong one, enduring pain quietly and then picking up and moving on. She probably felt she was protecting us, that she didn't want to burden us. What she didn't realize was that in doing so, she became for me unreal and unapproachable. I knew her outward self so well, but little else. But during the final stages of cancer, I knew I had to take the risk to break the pattern.

It happened one day as she lay in her recliner, the one place she felt some relief from the cancer's pain. She was weak from nausea and fatigue, but still clear minded. I waded in, still tentative and unsure, and began asking questions about her youth, her early years of marriage, and her faith. She didn't resist. She told me for the first time of her own loneliness at times, her questions, her broken dreams.

I felt the same thing I had with the pastor that Sunday morning. It was electric. I heard my mother's heart for the first time. I could feel the anger dissipate, replaced with compassion and a regret that I hadn't pursued her heart earlier. I even told her so. Sadly, there was no sequel to our conversation. She quickly declined after that. Yet it's a moment I will treasure forever. I knew the mother I had never known. She had told me her story.

THE POWER OF HEARING STORIES

This is the power of hearing the stories of others, of having them confide in us, telling us the secrets that have burdened them, trusting us to love them anyway. What actually happens to us in those moments? We first feel honored and privileged, being entrusted with something precious and unique. We have been considered worthy to hold another's heart. Such a sense of honor can come not only horizontally with others, but vertically with the Lord as well.

The psalmist asserted that "the LORD confides in those who fear him; he makes his covenant known to them" (Ps. 25:14 NIV). To know that we are being entrusted with the secrets of God's heart through his covenantal promises gives weight to our souls. We are being honored with the revelation. Jesus made a parallel statement to His disciples. He told them that He never saw them as mere servants, slaves who knew nothing of their master's business. Instead, He saw them as friends, as those who received the revelation the Father had given to Him, as those who heard His own heart (John 15:14–15). In a very real way, the Bible is the record of God's secrets, telling the story of His heart to us, hoping we will listen attentively, catch His heart, and be transformed by what He tells us.

But there is more here that impacts us. For in the listening, there is a connecting. This is what happened with my mother. The deep divide that Adam and Eve cut between themselves is now closing, and we feel a bond in place of the divide. As secrets are shared, the alienation we all feel is dismantled, not just for the one telling them but for the one hearing them as well. This ache for human connection is so intense, so throbbing, that it becomes the foundation of the most pervasive form of religious thought in history: pantheism. Here everything is seen as one; everything is connected. The force or power or spirit that underlies everything ties everyone together. But the fundamental inadequacy of pantheism is not in its focus on the ache to connect. It's with what the connection is made. We long to bond to *personality*, not an impersonal power or force. And that's

---

As secrets are shared, the alienation we all feel is dismantled, not just for the one telling them but for the one hearing them as well.

precisely what Jesus offers. In fact, it became the climax of His final prayer before His crucifixion: "Father, may they all be one as You are in Me and I am in You; may they be in Us, for by this unity the world will believe that You sent Me" (John 17:21).

The connection Jesus has with the Father is not just a sidebar in the story of the Bible. It's the central act from which the whole story of creation and redemption proceeds. For the Father and Son live unhindered, unashamed, without fear or jealousy or dysfunction, where they perfectly honor and serve each other. The life and love they share is not just the province of the divine; it's for us, as well. Jesus boldly envisioned this same type of connection among His followers, and then gave His life to make it possible. As we walk in this connection, others come to watch and see something extraordinary, and they, too, come to believe, so that the promise once given to Abraham to bless the whole world is now becoming a reality. In listening to others' stories, we can take a few halting steps toward all of this.

I have seen this happen, especially in the story groups I have led. In one of my recent groups is a man who has had his share of hardship, surviving sexual abuse as a teenager and a difficult divorce as an adult. But this is not his first time to participate in one of these groups. He is now on his third run. It's not that he needs more help in constructing his story. He can tell it with clarity, perspective, and hope. It's just that he finds the experience of listening to others healing in and of itself. He doesn't feel so alone.

Several years ago, another man joined these groups whose own story involved tragic emotional abuse and abandonment by his father. As someone who felt at the bottom of the pile, he was always intimidated by other men, convinced that they were far above him socially, economically, and spiritually. He felt stuck, fated to remain on the low rung of the ladder forever. But when he began to hear the stories of others, he was stunned. They were nothing like the constructs he had built of them in his mind. Instead, he found the ladder image shattering as he listened in on others' struggles, dismantling his own shame and connecting to other men for the first time.

But this growing connection doesn't just open out to others. It also opens upward to the Father. For what we experience horizontally, especially with our fathers, forms the emotional template for our experience with God vertically. That's why the woman whose father abandoned her as a child struggles to feel intimate with God, even though she believes God is with her. What she knows in her head still eludes her heart. That's why the man who was constantly criticized by his father struggles with even desiring God. Instead, he compulsively avoids Him or always feels guilty in His presence, not realizing that his experience of a condemning father has smeared the image of the true Father. Our fallen experiences dictate our true beliefs about God, whatever we may say we believe about Him. This divide can unexpectedly shift and narrow just in hearing the secrets of others.

But we need to remember that listening to others' stories is not some new therapy of this age. It's not pop psychology or narcissistic rambling. Augustine modeled it back in the fourth century in his *Confessions*, the first spiritual autobiography ever written. In it, he told the story of his pilgrimage to the Christian faith with such piercing honesty that it hurts at times to read it. No wonder it remains on many university lists as one of the top hundred books ever written. But the power of telling one's story is not just for intellectual giants like Augustine. It's for all of us. For once we come to faith, the most powerful story we have to give to others, besides the story of Jesus, is our own, with all of its sadness and woe, its aching wonder and buried glory. As others listen in, they are drawn to the radiance behind the shame, the beauty behind the brokenness, and as they are drawn to us, they can unconsciously be drawn to God. The divides disappear, and the connections begin.

SWITCHING SIDES

But with that, we have now switched sides from being the listeners to the ones telling the story, an equally transforming experience but with an entirely different feel. Here the surprise of hearing others reveal themselves shifts to the risk of revealing our own selves, the risk of being known. I remember this feeling so well in the pastoral ministry. As a preacher and spiritual leader, I felt that my job was to disseminate the truth and inspire my listeners to action and obedience. It was to know the truth and get it into my hearers. But the idea of being known like Augustine? The very thought of it sent terror through me. What I didn't understand then was that my terror was all part of the divide, that the mask I wore as a professional minister not only split me in terms of a public and private self; it split my head and my heart as well. And the villain in both cases was shame.

I have watched others face this same terror and reluctance. I clearly remember one story group where a man had to face the monster he had hidden in the closet all his life. With halting gaps and pauses, he related a tragic tale involving a distant father and then abuse at the hands of siblings and neighbors, both physical and sexual. When he finished, the terror of being known suddenly collided with the response of the men. It wasn't the feared condemnation or shame. It was sadness for him and compassion for the boy locked away all those years with this secret, the boy who'd never had the chance to be fathered, the boy who was brutalized instead of mentored by an older male. The relief of finally being known was intoxicating to him. It was so dramatic that he did something else that had once seemed unthinkable. He went home and told his wife the same story.

The inner revolution of being known feels just like that, a revolution. We are now pushing back against the very core of the tragic narrative that our first parents set into motion. Remember how Eve tried to grab at knowing on her own terms, detached from being known by God in relationship, no longer trusting him for the good. The decision to separate knowing from being known lies at the heart of the divide. It also lies at the heart of the cure, for we can't enter the realm of being known by more analysis or understanding. All of that is where the problem lies in the first place. It's not that knowledge or concepts are in and of themselves wrong or even evil. Far from it. It's just that the energy behind them is so often avoidance, fear, control. We can never close the divide by simply trying to understand it more, by even reading this book again. We have to let go. We have to trust. We have to allow ourselves to be known. It's a counterintuitive leap that is only understood after the jump.

We are now back to the leap of faith that Indiana Jones had to make as he looked out over the gaping chasm. He was not going to bully his way through this one. He was going to have to do something contrary to his whole character and personality. He was going to have to trust and let go. Only after that first step out did he see the bridge that was out there all along. Only as we leap in telling our story will we find the bridge to cross the chasm ourselves.

The decision to separate knowing from being known lies at the heart of the divide. It also lies at the heart of the cure.

Paul carved out the same distinction between knowing and being known in his rebuttal to the Corinthian church. They claimed to have found the true knowledge of the faith and the proper way to live it out, especially as it relates to the explosive issue of eating meat sacrificed to pagan idols. Paul's response was that their understanding of knowledge was misguided from the beginning: "Just because a person presumes to have some bit of knowledge, that person doesn't necessarily have the right kind of knowledge" (1 Cor. 8:2). Knowledge for fallen humanity almost always ends up as a status symbol, a power play, whereby the one who is in the know uses it to stand over those who aren't. And such knowledge always leads to pride and, in the church, it leads to one of the most destructive of all sins, spiritual pride. If we think we know something that makes us feel we are better than others, we have only shown how duped we are.

And that takes us to the surprising twist in the next verse, Paul's understanding of true knowledge: "But if someone loves God, *it is certain that* God has already known that one" (v. 3). In this tight aphorism, we find two important ideas. First, it's ultimately not about our knowledge of God or correct theology or proper ethics. The true sign that we have any understanding of the living God and what he has done for us in Christ is that we love Him, that our hearts are drawn to Him, that we ache to be with Him, that we are letting go of all the other false loves in our lives.

But that leads to the second point. Who is the person who loves God? It is the person known by God. It is the one who feels the eyes of the Father looking at him, looking straight into him, and feels no guilt or shame but only the compassion of He who longs to draw us to Himself. Only the one who feels known like this can truly know. Right here is the undoing of Eve's deed, the un-choosing of Eve's choice. This is how we enter that second tale of redemption. It's also how we become whole and undivided.

A FINAL SURPRISE

But taking the risk to reveal our story opens us up for another unexpected surprise. We start seeing ourselves through the eyes of others, namely, those who reenvision our own experiences, reinterpreting and recasting them in a new light. And what we feel is something that once seemed inconceivable: delight, instead of shame. The parts of our heart that we once hid in terror become the very reasons why others love us. This new reality is so startling that we scarcely know what to do with it. But of this we can be sure: it plunges a sword right into the heart of shame, mortally wounding it forever.

The dramatic nature of this reimaging is powerfully portrayed in *The King's Speech*, the true story of Bertie, the Duke of York, who unexpectedly inherits the throne of England after his older brother abdicates. There is only one problem: he is a horrendous stutterer. The prospect of becoming a king is his worst nightmare. He will be shamed before the listening world as a king with no voice, right when England, about to enter World War II, needs a voice the most. In one poignant moment with his wife, he breaks into tears, lamenting, "I'm not a king. I'm not a king." His terror comes to a head in an exchange with his speech therapist, Lionel Logue, the day before the coronation service. Lionel prods him into an angry outburst by plopping himself down on the throne, trivializing this sacred symbol of power. In his rage, Bertie quits stuttering, demands that Lionel get off the throne, and asserts that he has a voice to be heard. Lionel's response is striking: "Yes, you do. You have such perseverance, Bertie. You're the bravest man I know. You'll make a bloody good king." [4] What we see next in Bertie's eyes is a look of stunned confusion. Lionel has just taken Bertie's deepest flaw and reimaged it as his greatest asset. All Bertie can see is the shaming disability that pricks him again and again in every conversation, every interaction. What he doesn't see is what he could never see on his own, that the battle to find his own voice has slowly chiseled him into a man worthy of being a king. Only the eyes of another could reinterpret this, turning shame into triumph.

I had my own watershed moment of reimaging a couple of years ago, one that left me just as stunned. As I neared the end of my work as a high school teacher and coach, I knew God was calling me out as an author and speaker. But the sheer reality of so many unknowns ahead kept me tentative and ambivalent. The climactic moment came when I gathered six friends in my living room, friends who were to become the starting board of a new ministry we had dreamed about for some time. I imagine they were expecting me to lay out the plans to move ahead. Instead, I sputtered and retracted, saying I wasn't ready for this right now, that we should wait and see what would happen on other fronts. I ended my little speech with a question I considered rhetorical: "Is everybody with me on this?"

I'll never forget the first response. One man, whose usual demeanor is friendly and encouraging, raised himself up off the chair and forcefully uttered one word: *NO*. He couldn't accept my stalling or retreating. The time to start was now, and I needed to get to work. Then, one by one, each friend in that room took his turn and told me basically the same thing. My proposal to stall was universally vetoed. I was stunned speechless. All I could see in that moment was my own anxiety and fear. They saw something else, a man with God's call who needed to go and be obedient. There was nothing for me to do that afternoon but acquiesce and submit. I felt the power of reimaging that afternoon in a way that has changed everything for me. Without their vote of confidence, the ministry would never have started, much less gotten this far.

This sort of reimaging has many other strands and variations. It can happen when a teacher calls out something in a student that was previously untapped, or when a coach pushes an athlete because of the potential he sees inside. It can occur when a boss promotes an unsuspecting employee, seeing in him latent talent. It can happen when a father speaks words of blessing to his adolescent son, pulling him up into manhood, or when a wife reimages the shame or sadness in her husband, loving him precisely at the point of devastation.

When each of our daughters turned sixteen, Heidi and I invited over a small group of women who each had a significant relationship with that daughter. One by one they commented on what they saw in her, sharing their hopes and prayers for her. Each daughter felt seen through the eyes of others, with words that we hoped as parents would nourish her as a woman in the journey ahead.

This sort of reimaging now touches so near to the central nerve of what Jesus longs to do in our lives. To say that He wants to help us get rid of a few bad habits is pitifully insufficient. Equally inadequate is the vague idea that His plan is to make us into better men and women. Jesus just doesn't want to change our behavior; He wants to change how we see ourselves. He wants to stain us with the truth, invading our stories, and calling us out of them into his, in a way that permanently alters our whole sense of being. The reimaging

**The parts of our heart that we
once hid in terror become the very
reasons why others love us.**

I experienced with my friends in that decisive moment in the living room is something Jesus continues to do for me personally.

After a particularly turbulent week trying to begin this new ministry, I had felt like giving everything up and going back into the high school classroom. I awoke early one morning, hungry, aching, struggling to listen. In the middle of my musings on some scripture, this is what I suddenly heard from Jesus: *"Fix your eyes on Me."* And then an image came to me of mountain climbing. Jesus was on the next ledge up, holding the rope, and He was looking down at me, speaking those words in a confident and encouraging tone. I was in a precipitous spot on the rock face where I couldn't go back down. The only way forward was to ascend. So I looked up into His eyes and felt how He saw me, as the man who can climb this mountain roped up with Him leading the way. I also saw that this is a part of how Jesus is drawing me out as a man, as someone who can take on the task given to him and actually do it. And if He believes that I can climb this mountain, then I need to believe it also. Right after I had this image, I opened up to the end of Habakkuk, for I knew there was something parallel there. This is what I read: "The Sovereign LORD is my strength; he makes my feet like the feet of a deer, he enables me to go on the heights" (3:21 NIV). I was stunned. There it was. The same basic image. Jesus wasn't just encouraging me in the image to persevere, although it certainly was encouraging. He wasn't just trying to get my eyes off of the difficulties of the present work, although I certainly had to do that to look into His eyes. He was doing something more. I could feel it as I looked into His eyes and connected with Him. I could feel what He felt toward me. It was another watershed moment. I had felt the eyes of Him who holds all authority in heaven and on earth, reimaging me, telling me, *I am with you. You can do this.* I closed my Bible and took on the day. It was time to climb. I was ready.

PRAYER:

Father, I come running to You. I am so weary of carrying around the false self. I am so exhausted from hiding my sins and burdens. I ache to connect to others and to You. You created me this way, and yet so many things have cut me off from that connection. Help me begin to tell my story, to confess my secret sins, and to share my darkest burdens. I am terrified by what others may think, yet I know this is the way forward. I have to begin to trust others and in so doing, learn to trust You more. Give me the opportunity to bear the burdens of others also and to pray for them as they share their secret sins. And teach me to see myself the way You see me. All I see is my sin and my shame. Yet I know that this is all forgiven, that Jesus took my sin and my shame. I want to see You seeing me. Only then will I see You the way you truly are.

FATHER: *My child, you are at the edge of a great discovery. You are not just allowing others to love you. You are also learning how to remain in My Son, how to stay in My presence. As you open your heart to others, you will find it opening to Me in new ways also. This is how you will learn to stay rooted and grounded in the love I have for you. This is how you will experience the fullness of My Son and become the person I have made you to be. I know you. Rest in that for now.*

QUESTIONS FOR JOURNALING AND DISCUSSION

1. Select one quote that you found especially helpful or insightful. Describe what you got out of it.

2. Describe a time when you heard a person's story told in a vulnerable way. What do you remember about the story? How did it change the way you felt about that person? What were you feeling while the story was being told? When it finished?

3. James 5:16 and Galatians 6:2 call us to a life of mutual confession and burden bearing. Have you ever told your story to someone else? If so, what was it like? If not, what has kept you from doing this? Take the reverse situation now. Has anyone ever done this with you? What was that experience like?

4. What we experience horizontally, especially with our fathers, forms the emotional template for our experience with God vertically. Comment on how you have seen this play out in your own life.

5. Have you ever had someone—a friend, coach, parent, mentor— reimage who you thought you were, calling out things in you that you couldn't see yourself? Describe that experience and how it impacted you.

6. Jesus wants to come and personally reimage each of us by the power of the Holy Spirit. All of the great statements in Scripture—that we have been forgiven, washed clean, and given the righteousness of Jesus, and that we are beloved by the Father

and a delight to Him—can be ours as we let Jesus enter our fallen stories and reimage us the way He sees us. What does such a prospect stir up in you? What did the last story in the chapter stir up in you?

PART III

CLOSING THE DIVIDE

What the Journey Feels Like

Neo, sooner or later you're going to realize, just as I did, there's a difference between knowing the path and walking the path.

—Morpheus, in *The Matrix* [1]

But it seems to me now clear which is the road that we must take. The westward road seems easiest. Therefore it must be shunned. It will be watched. Too often the Elves have fled that way. Now at this last we must take a hard road, a road unforeseen. There lies our hope, if hope it be. To walk into peril—to Mordor.

—Elrond, in *The Fellowship of the Ring* [2]

"Can this be faith?" he thought, afraid to believe in his happiness. "I thank Thee, my God!" [Levin] murmured, gulping down the sobs that were rising within him, and with both hands wiping away the tears that filled his eyes.

—Leo Tolstoy, *Anna Karenina* [3]

I have come home at last! This is my real country! I belong here. This is the land I have been looking for all my life, though I never knew it till now. The reason why we loved the old Narnia is that it sometimes looked a little like this.

—Jewel the Unicorn, in *The Last Battle* [4]

So bow down under God's strong hand; then when the time comes, God will lift you up.

—1 Peter 5:6

THE DESCENT

Submit to death, death of your ambitions and favorite wishes every day and death of your whole body in the end; submit with every fiber of your being, and you will find eternal life. Keep back nothing. . . . Nothing in you that has not died will ever be raised from the dead.

—C. S. Lewis [1]

When I was in college, my parents loaded the whole family into a twenty-seven-foot mobile home and drove us off to do something completely novel—explore the Wild West. We spent the next three weeks enthralled by one sight after another: the sweeping fields of the Great Plains, the iconic sculpturing of Mount Rushmore, the fuming sprays of Yellowstone Park, and the chiseled cirques of the Tetons. It felt as though we were entering one wonderland after another. But there was one final stop on this trip, one we had all anticipated perhaps more than any other. It was a place each of us had seen in books and pictures, but none of that could have ever prepared us for the actual sight. As we neared the appointed destination, we steered the mobile home into the parking lot and jumped out onto the pavement, edgy with excitement. Rushing right up to the edge, we caught our first glimpse. The plateau on which we stood abruptly fell away for several thousand feet, with no fences, no rails to guard us from the airy expanse ahead. The panorama before us left us momentarily speechless: a vast array of red and orange coloring; jagged landscapes mottled with cloud and sunlight; and layered rock deeply cloven by unseen water. We were looking at one of the biggest holes on earth. We were looking at the Grand Canyon.

The hole is so wide that it stretches at points nearly eighteen miles across. It is so deep that you must drop an entire mile of elevation to get from the rim to the bottom. The sheer immensity of the whole thing had no previous category, no comparison, in our minds. But this was only the beginning. We weren't there just to look at the Grand Canyon. We were there to explore it, to feel it, to experience it. And there's only one way to do that. You have to go down.

That next morning, my brother, sister, and I took a few supplies and began the seven-mile descent to the bottom. As the trail dropped steeply, making endless switchbacks, the rocks changed in texture and hue as sweeping views continued to open out to us. But the weather changed also. What started out as a crisp August morning turned into a sultry summer day, with temperatures soaring

---

This is where we are now. We all face a journey, something to enter, not just read about.

into the nineties. We were now tired and sweating, but determined to press on.

After crossing a lower plain nestled down in the canyon, the final descent began. The rocks took on a grayish-blue tone, denser and more ancient than we had seen before. Finally, after dropping more than five thousand feet, exhausted and bruised, I took off my hiking boots and plunged my bare feet into the icy Colorado River, a sign of triumph.

I tell of this journey not as a quaint travelogue but as a metaphor. For what lies before us now is a journey. Up to this point, I have tried to give you a general briefing on the divide and some strategies for tackling it. It's like sitting at your kitchen table, looking through picture books of the Grand Canyon and pulling out the trail maps. But the books are not the reality. The maps are not the journey. At some point, you have to go there, get on the trail, and descend. Whatever the actual experience is like, good or bad, it will be very different from sitting in the comfort of your kitchen. This is where we are now. We all face a journey, something to enter, not just read about. But this is no Grand Canyon. This is a Grand Divide. It, too, is a massive hole blown in the psyche of the human race, a divide so wide and deep that it may seem impossible to cross. Yet cross it we must if we are to close it. And the direction to do so is the same as that of the Grand Canyon. It's down; it's a descent.

THE PERIL OF DESCENDING

The path to close the divide between our heads and hearts will require more from us than we knew we could possibly give because this descent is not geographical—it's spiritual. It's a descent into the sins to which we have become blind, into the memories we push down, and into the fears we don't understand. It's pushing down through the layers we have wrapped around ourselves, layers of self-protection and masking, of learned responses and patterned thinking, layers that have helped us survive but can never make us alive. It's a descent to strip all of that away so that we can discover who we really are and what we are supposed to do with our lives. If you feel some level of trepidation at these words, there is good reason. This is not a journey easily chosen or comfortably made. There will be points where we feel we can't go on, where we have had enough, where it will be maddeningly tempting to go back to the known and familiar. There will be other points of such utter confusion and bewilderment that the darkness will feel like quicksand in which we are slowly sinking. Why even bother with such a perilous descent? Why even consider such a journey? Ultimately, there's only one reason. It's not the journey; it's who is asking us to go. It's Jesus Himself: "If any of you want to walk My path, you're going to have to deny yourself. You'll have to take up your cross every day and follow Me" (Luke 9:23). Denial and death are the descent. That's the only way we can follow Him.

Paul certainly followed the Master when he penned these striking words: "May I never boast except in the cross of our Lord Jesus Christ, through which the world has been crucified to me, and I to the world" (Gal. 6:14 NIV). Paul's sense of denial and death was so pervasive that the most humiliating, disgusting symbol of that time—the cross—was the one thing that he took pride in. And with that inversion, he descended further. The systems of this world—with its hierarchies and philosophies, its relentless hunger for wealth and fame, its corrupting power, and its sucking narcissism—were the very things he became dead to. They had no pull on him. They were, in fact, as disgusting to him as the cross is to the world. This was a categorical renouncing of the old ways of humanity. They can't be tinkered with, adjusted, or retooled. We must die to them. And the only way to get there is down.

Despite what may seem so hard to swallow, this is really no surprise. When Jesus opened His ministry, traveling from town to town in Galilee, his proclamation began with a call to death: "Repent, for the kingdom of heaven is at hand" (Matt. 4:17). To repent is to die to the old ways so we can follow the new ones of the kingdom. Jesus made it perfectly clear from the very beginning what this was all about.

One of the great poems of all time, Dante's *Divine Comedy*, assumes the same directional orientation. The book opens with Dante the poet becoming Dante the pilgrim. Riddled with error and sin, he finds himself lost in the woods of life. Seeing the Mount of Joy in the distance, he goes there and tries to ascend its steep hill, only to fail in the attempt. He then learns from his guide, Virgil, that he must first descend through hell itself before he can ascend. Dante gets it. He has to start by going down.

I once heard the story of a Stealth fighter plane performing training maneuvers one night. It was flying low to the ground at a fast rate of speed when the pilot noticed an upcoming elevation rise on his radar. He instinctively pulled up on the throttle to gain altitude, and with that the plane suddenly crashed into the ground, killing everyone on board. When the black box was found and examined, it was discovered that the pilot had made a terrible error. He had pulled up without looking at the rest of his instruments. The

---

The things we think will give us life destroy us. The things we hope will fill our hearts corrupt us. The things we trust to make us happy deceive us.

plane had been flying upside down for some time, and he had just forgotten. Pulling up was actually going down. What the pilot assumed would save the plane destroyed it.

This is such an apt illustration for what lies before us. If it all seems upside down or backward, it's not. We are the ones who have it backward and are flying upside down. The things we think will give us life destroy us. The things we hope will fill our hearts corrupt us. The things we trust to make us happy deceive us. Perhaps a countermove is what we need, something unexpected, something we wouldn't have thought of. Perhaps Jesus' call to die is really His call to come alive. And with that understanding, our courage is bolstered. We're ready to take some steps forward, even knowing that the way down will be difficult. But what exactly are these difficulties? What will we have to encounter?

One of the most persistent of all myths is one in which a dragon must be fought and slain. From *Beowulf* to Saint George to *The Hobbit*, it's an image that reappears in many cultures and contexts. The dragon may hold a princess hostage. He may sit on stolen treasure. He may block a city entry. Whatever the details, he is an obstacle that must be overcome. But there is only one way to deal with a dragon. You can't negotiate with him or sweet-talk him or bribe him. You have to face him and slay him. That's what this descent is all about. We are going to be facing dragons and slaying them.

THE DRAGON OF IDOLATRY

This first "dragon" is one that constantly overwhelmed the Israelites throughout the Old Testament: idolatry. In the Bible, an idol is a substitute for the living God, an exchange of the Creator for the created. We are not much different from those Israelites. All of the things on which we hook ourselves—our addictions and dependencies—these function as our idols, our God substitutes. An addictive personality is not some special type; it's a description of the human race. We are all addicts. We all have addictive personalities.

Adam and Eve started the whole mess by swapping intimacy with the Creator for a piece of fruit. It sounds insane. It *is* insane. But idols don't come to us in a way that feels insane. They present themselves in the same way they appeared to our first parents, with voices that woo and entice, wrapping their spell around us, seducing us until we can't think clearly. And instead of a single piece of fruit, we have an endless array to choose from.

I once asked a class of adults to help me make up a list of possible addictions. Hands went up immediately. I was peppered with answers, and I hurriedly wrote them on the whiteboard. In a few minutes, the entire board was crammed full. The list feels so endless because anything in God's good creation can become idolatrous. We take that good and twist it into evil: eating becomes gluttony; sex becomes pornography; money becomes greed; medication becomes drug abuse. And then there are the deeper addictions: purpose becomes blind ambition; love becomes people pleasing; discipline becomes drivenness. Why do we twist the good like this? Because our idols provide us with immediate relief, giving us a lift, helping us hold our lives together, even providing a measure of meaning and focus. All of these are things that God also promises, but we have to learn to trust Him for them. Precisely here lies the allure of all idolatry: instant relief, no trusting or waiting required. We can turn to the idol whenever we desire, or so we think. But we are deceived.

When we choose an idol to handle the hardship and sadness of life, the momentary comfort it provides feels pleasant at first, then needed, and finally indispensable. We are hooked. On a fishing trip in the Quetico Provincial Park of Ontario, I once caught a pike with a jig that had multiple hooks. Somehow this poor fellow got several of them caught inside his mouth and on his face. He was a tangled mess. Since we were not keeping pike, I had to do minor surgery to remove all the hooks before I could throw him back. Our hearts are something like this unfortunate fish, hooked into a tangled mess. And with our hearts hooked, we now lose the power to choose our idols. They have chosen us. Our wills become impotent to *do* what's right even when we *know* what's right. So when we come to believe in Jesus, in His forgiveness and love for us, these truths initially capture our hearts, but they struggle to make much headway into our daily lives. What we believe to be true feels split off from what we choose in life. Paul had this same struggle in his own journey: "I can determine that I am going to do good, but I don't do it; instead, I end up living out the evil that I decided not to do" (Rom. 7:19). The guilt or shame we feel over this divided state of affairs only adds to the split. More information about the truth doesn't help either. It deepens the rift even further. Powerless, we despair of ever changing.

STRIPPING OFF

Idols are fearsome dragons that must be slain to keep moving in our descent to close our divided heads and hearts. But how do we slay the beast that seems to have conquered us? One word: stripping. Slaying this beast requires stripping off the idols, intentionally, relentlessly, one by one, in whatever way we can manage or understand at the time. But this is only half the battle. When we strip off an idol, often we don't feel better. We feel worse. All of the unanesthetized pain, all of the unfulfilled longing, all of the ungrieved losses we have pushed down, now bubble back up to the surface. Without our drug of choice at hand, the temptation to go back to it may feel over-whelming, drowning out the courage we felt to strip it off in the first place. To keep going, our resolve will need to stiffen, and we will have to learn an old word in a new way: *trust*.

Over and over, through story, proverb, and command, the Bible asks us to trust God. With our hearts aching and longing, we now understand. This is trusting. It's banking our hearts and hopes on Him, knowing that if He doesn't come through in our pain and confusion, all is lost. And now something unexpected happens. Without our awareness or conscious effort, what we have desired starts to happen: the divide is closing. Trust is no longer a nice idea in our file cabinet of biblical truths. It's a tactile, visceral reality born out of desperation and need.

One of my friends is at this junction on his own descent. He already stripped off the idols of sex, alcohol, and food some time ago. Now he is pushing back into the deeper idols of approval and fame. The voluntary stripping has left him keenly aware of the terrible ache of abandonment he felt as a child. The pull to go back and scavenge for the old idols feels irresistible at times. But like a good soldier, he is determined to keep going, resolved to slay this beast. He told me recently that he is learning to sit in the pain and trust that Jesus will come for him. For him this means sitting alone for long periods with his heart aching and the Scriptures open. He has had to face the terror that, if all of this isn't true, he will be undone. His courageous choice to trust is teaching him something that comes

---

This is trusting. It's banking our hearts and hopes on Him, knowing that if He doesn't come through in our pain and confusion, all is lost.

to us no other way. Pain will never kill us. It's the avoidance of pain that kills us. And my friend is seeing Jesus show up in the pain, proving His promises, closing the divide. He is slaying the dragon.

A FORCED STRIPPING

But despite all of our needed efforts, ultimately God will have to come and do the final surgery, removing the hooks in His time, in His way. I wish I could offer more in terms of help or advice. I'm afraid I can't. We're not dealing here with a method or technique. We're dealing with the Holy One of the universe, who will not be reduced to a formula for our control. How He will deal with us is as unique as our fingerprints. What I can offer is a recounting of how He has performed the surgery on me.

One of my most sensible idols was exercise, especially long-distance running. I discovered it in a collegiate fitness class when I ran nearly two miles in twelve minutes. It was something that came naturally to me with my body build. After college the running became more pronounced and repetitive. I found that it helped with my chronic depression, allowing me to feel better. But soon what was helpful became mandatory. Every day became structured around "getting the run in." What made this idol even more compelling is that it hooked me right at that old lie about athletics: that somehow physical prowess in a sport would make me feel like a man.

During the progression of my captivity to this idol, I got hooked to a secondary one. I found that the more I exercised, the more I could eat. Dinner became not just an enjoyable moment in the day, but a time when I could gorge, going back for thirds and even fourths. The pleasure attached to eating became a substitute for the disconnect I felt from others. I exchanged intimacy for gluttony.

During family reunions, I wasn't so interested in reconnecting as I was getting that long run in on the beach so I could eat a massive dinner. The next day I would wake up, knowing I needed to work off the previous night's indulgence. It now became a vicious cycle, one over which I had little control. I had lost the power to choose. What was so confusing was the context: I was trapped here during my years as a pastor and Bible teacher. I could speak the truth, but I couldn't feel it. I couldn't choose it. I was a split personality.

To unhook myself here wasn't easy. I had to confess to others that I was an addict. I had to strip off what I could by managing my food intake and limiting my exercise. But even with all of this, I found the hooks deeply planted. As in so many of these cases, God had to do surgery, and it happened in a dramatic way. I had been having back issues for a couple of years, and on a hunch from a chiropractor, I ended up one day in the office of a hip doctor. The X-rays revealed the source of my pain. I had developed minor arthritis after years of running, due to a congenital bone defect in my hip. The upshot: quit running or face a hip replacement. I walked out stunned. After all my years of running, what would I be without it? What would life be like? I remember feeling grief and then tears welling up as I passed a runner on the drive home from the doctor. I felt as if I were being asked to part with a lover or say good-bye to a dying friend. Leaving our idols always feels like this. But in God's cunning way, He was taking the pliers and pulling the hook out where I had repeatedly failed. Soon after this, however, I felt something completely unexpected: relief. I was relieved that I didn't have to go and run, that my running didn't define me, that I could now take on new adventures. What at first had felt like death now became life. I had rediscovered my power to choose, and with it, my power to choose God.

This type of forced stripping is movingly chronicled in Tolstoy's epic *War and Peace*. The main character, Pierre, spends most of the book living in unparalleled wealth and luxury. He also spends that same time in a frantic search for meaning in life, trying to escape the despair that nearly sends him to suicide. When Napoleon invades Moscow, Pierre suddenly becomes a prisoner of war, forced to march in inhumane conditions, walking barefoot with horrific sores on his feet, smelling the odors of death and decay everywhere. He is stripped of his wealth, his dignity, his titles, his possessions, everything. And there, in the last of all places he expected, in watching and listening to a peasant soldier around the campfire, he finds meaning. He finds happiness. He finds God.

The human heart is so constructed that it is going to stick to something, much like flypaper or Velcro. And if we don't attach to the living God, we will attach to the endless idols around us. But once the Great Surgeon has does His work, that part of our heart is free again, free to receive the truth and live in it. He is helping us slay this dragon—but more dragons await.

THE DRAGON OF SHAME

The stripping off of our idols will keep us descending further on our path to close the divide, where we will now encounter an even fiercer dragon, one that seems impervious to all swords and spears. It is the dragon of shame. Shame radically distorts the way we see ourselves, the way we see everything. We become ashamed of our bodies, ashamed of our weaknesses, ashamed of our failures, ashamed of our pasts, ashamed of our hearts—even ashamed of our shame. Shame now becomes the unmentionable subject. To even speak of it resurrects the shame.

I recently taught a class in which I described how the voice of shame defines us. You would have thought I was talking about the end of the world. I could feel a heaviness descend on the class with that distraught look in their eyes. Why the reaction? Because calling it out touches the throbbing center of our fallenness.

One man who has courageously battled through many of his own idols was finally able to put his finger on the throbbing center of his own pain. It was a very specific moment when he was nine years old. The craze among children back then was the TV show *The Mickey Mouse Club*. He had wanted to be just like one of the Mouseketeers, as the child stars on the program were called. The costumes they wore were available in stores, and when he was finally able to get one, he wore it with pride. He was just like the famous boys on TV.

All of that changed the day he wore the Mouseketeer suit on an excursion with his father. Meeting one of his father's friends, they struck up a casual conversation. But in the middle of it, his father gave a disparaging look at his son, acting embarrassed over the costume. The boy was shattered. His delight in the outfit became shock and then shame. He couldn't wait to get home and take it off, vowing never to wear it again. At that moment, something inside him shifted forever. He began to see himself as the son who was funda- mentally flawed, who would never be able to please his father. The fact that his father was a professional athlete only made the issue worse. He knew before he even attempted sports that he could never live up to his father's standards, so he never tried.

This story is so exemplary of what shame does to us. It can come through anyone who has some level of power and status over us. What that person does or says in that shaming moment becomes defining for who we are, covering us with a slime that colors every- thing we feel and think. The instigator can be a sneering father, an overbearing coach, a manipulative mother, a condemning teacher, a bullying student—anyone whose voice has sway and influence.

But shame doesn't even have to have a voice. Without another voice encouraging and affirming us, we are easily swept away into endless comparisons with others. Heidi has wrestled with this type of shame for much of her life. It wasn't one defining voice. It was just the absence of any protecting, nurturing voice. And without that, she felt constantly assaulted with comparisons. They started in middle school, when she realized that her clothes were subpar. Her parents weren't able to afford nice dresses for her, and she never felt that she measured up to the other girls in class. The same thing happened in athletics. She vividly remembers going to play softball on one of the park recreation teams in the fifth grade. As she arrived for practice, one of the more athletic girls blurted out, "Oh no! Now we're going to lose." That sense of never being good enough carried over into her attempts to play lacrosse in high school. It was also that way with her looks, as she never felt as pretty as other girls. Shame always puts us on an endless merry-go-round of comparisons, leaving us reeling and emotionally nauseated.

But the worst part of shame is its commanding power. It issues only one order, blaring it out over and over: *Cover and hide. Cover and hide. Cover and hide.* We feel compelled to obey—and when we do, the dividing starts. We can no longer enjoy being known for who we are. In fact, the very possibility of that seems as remote as another galaxy. Whoever we are, shame screams at us that we are not enough. So we must split ourselves, projecting a false persona to avoid further shame and hiding our truest selves. That hiding can

What that person does or says in that shaming moment becomes defining for who we are, covering us with a slime that colors everything we feel and think.

take on a very physical context when the shame is over our bodies. One man told me how he suffered from acne on his chest and a weak upper body during his high school years. Even though he was a standout basketball player, he was reluctant to take off his shirt during team practices. When the coach called the players to separate into shirts and skins, he dreaded the possibility of being put on the skins team, exposing to others what he thought would bring him ridicule. What he felt in that moment of dread is what we all feel about shame, physical or otherwise. The thought of exposure terrifies us, so we cover and hide.

FIGHTING BY REVEALING

The dragon of shame must be squarely faced and bitterly fought. At times we will be thrusting our swords at him with all our might. At other times, it will feel as if we are wrestling him in the mud and muck, for this is a mortal combat in which one side will be the victor and the other the vanquished. There is no middle ground. And the only way to come out as the victor is to defy shame's compelling voice and do the opposite: *unmask and reveal.* Remember: descending always requires a countermove, the opposite of our normal habits. It will always feel risky, edgy, precarious.

How do you make this happen? You just start. You start with a friend, a pastor, a counselor, anyone. Start with what you know you are hiding and go from there. For some of us, there will be many layers of shame to push through. Remember the man with the Mouseketeers costume. It took him several years of counseling along with the encouragement of others before he was even able to pull up that story. It lay deeply buried and carefully protected. The uncovering and revealing will lead to unforeseen shifts, pulling our fractured souls together in ways we have never known. We may even do something completely unthinkable before now: openly tell our stories to help others.

Matt is the chairman of the ministry board under which I work. His story of sadness and shame began as a boy of twelve with a father who died of a heart attack and a mother who simply did not know how to handle grief. Matt dealt with the terrible loss in a way so many young men do: he got angry. Even though he tried to conceal it behind a carefully constructed "happy" life, his high school buddies would joke about his occasional angry outbursts.

But it was no joke after he got married. The stresses of work and family would pull him into a black hole, where he would respond with outbursts of rage that would terrorize his wife and children. This is the life he carefully hid. In the outside world, he was known as a successful businessman and church leader, respected and even revered. But after Matt began to reveal his rage and grief with those he trusted, he was eventually able to do something incredibly courageous, something once inconceivable to him. One Sunday he got up in front of the entire church and told his story. The effect on the congregation was electric. The effect on Matt was more healing. The divide between his head and his heart was closing.

The Scriptures give us some intriguing glimpses into fighting shame. One of the most arresting comes from Hebrews 12:2: "Let us fix our eyes of Jesus, the author and perfecter of our faith, who for the joy set before him endured the cross, scorning its shame, and sat down at the right hand of the throne of God" (NIV). Jesus is pictured here as the great pioneer of the faith, hacking out a new pathway for all humanity. And the pathway looks familiar, a descent into the horror of the cross, followed by an ascent into the joy awaiting Him. But in His descent to bear the evil of the human race, Jesus did something unprecedented with shame: He scorned it. He mocked it, refusing to let it define Him. He was going to be defined by His Father, even if everything around Him at the crucifixion was screaming mockery, abandonment, and pain. He fought the dragon of shame by doing something revolutionary. He shamed shame itself. See, the power of shame comes from allowing others to define us—by their words, their thoughts, their judgments. Jesus simply refused to do this and took the sting of shame away once and for all. He refused to give shame that power. Only what the Father thought mattered.

We are asked to follow Jesus here, for He is the trailblazer of a new humanity, beckoning us to come. What does it mean to follow Him? Shame makes us cower, roll over, and admit defeat. We feel branded, imprisoned in whatever sentence shame gives us. But to shame shame itself, to scorn it, means to get back up. It means taking back the power we have given others to define us, standing on our feet again, and entrusting ourselves to the Father as Jesus did. He alone can define us. Only what He says matters in the end because only He knows who we really are. This is the mortal wound we can inflict on this dragon, sending him into the throes of death.

THE GREAT DRAGON HIMSELF

One last dragon remains to be encountered on this descent to close the head and heart. But now we move from metaphor to actuality, from symbol to reality. Early depictions of dragons didn't have wings and scales like the ones we often see today. They were more like serpents, similar perhaps to what Eve encountered. We are now coming to that serpent, the Great Dragon, the one whose power and might instigated the fracturing of the human race. We come to Satan himself.

The Scriptures picture him not just as a serpent but also as a vicious, ravenous lion on the prowl, seeking someone to devour (1 Peter 5:8). The ferocity of his roar was something ever on Jesus' mind. In the model prayer He gave us, the Lord's Prayer, the last request was aimed at deliverance from this ruthless beast (Matt. 6:13). Why? Because behind the evil in the human soul, behind the world's systems that legitimize and propagate that evil, lies evil personified: the evil one himself. If he is the mastermind behind our fall from God, if he is the underlying source of our fracturing, we can count on him to oppose our attempts at closing the divide. It will be like turning a boat directly into gale-force winds after gliding along with it for hours. All of a sudden we will feel his power in a startling way. We are not going along with his game plan anymore. The bottom line: every step will be fiercely challenged.

We have felt his opposition already with the previous dragons we have fought. He is behind the spell that our idols cast over us, seducing and blinding us. He is behind the sting of shame, as he was in the garden, mocking and condemning us. Fighting through idolatry and shame will sooner or later bring us face-to-face with the Great Dragon. And his chief weapon is something so commonplace, so pedestrian, that we can scarcely believe its power. He doesn't tear and mangle with claws or incinerate with fire from his mouth. He uses something much simpler, yet much more perverse. He uses a lie.

THE GREAT DRAGON'S WEAPON OF CHOICE

Jesus pointed this out in His disputation with the Pharisees. He denounced these respected leaders as children of the devil and then offered this incisive comment about the devil himself: "He started out as a killer, and he cannot tolerate truth because he is void of anything true. At the core of his character, he is a liar; everything he speaks originates in these lies because he is the father of lies" (John 8:44). Jesus intimates that behind all the lies that we believe is a liar. But the enemy's lies are not just intended to deceive. They are out to murder and assassinate. He is a killer, and he kills through his lies.

One of the best pictures of this, strangely enough, is from an animated film for children. *The Lion King* portrays the consummate satanic figure in the character of Scar, brother to the mighty king Mufasa. Scar concocts a plot to dethrone his brother and kill the heir so he can gain the throne himself. He dupes Mufasa's son, Simba, then just a cub, into walking into a canyon, and then sets off an antelope stampede through it. When Mufasa rushes in to rescue his son, he is trampled to death. Scar finishes off the job by insinuating to Simba that he is to blame for Mufasa's death. Simba is left in shock, horrified that he has murdered his own father and crushed by shame because it's his fault. So he runs away, trying to forget his past, burying his identity as a son and his destiny as the king. But as the film progresses, Simba makes the courageous choice to return home and stand up to Scar. As he learns the truth of what really happened to his father, he makes this decisive statement: "Why should I believe you, Scar? Everything you ever told me was a lie."[2] Simba finally understands. Lying is his uncle's native language. Scar is the real murderer, the one who took his father out and nearly took him out.

**But the enemy's lies are not just
intended to deceive. They are out
to murder and assassinate.**

There's a part of me that is intrigued with the striking parallels between Scar and Satan. But another part of me steps back and wonders: *This is an animated film, not real life. Isn't this a bit overdramatic to suggest we are being murdered by an evil power?* It does seem that way until I think about the lies I have believed over the years, the ones I have chronicled in this book that slowly suffocated my heart. Like Simba, I also believed that everything was my fault. I, too, ran away and hid until I began to despair of life itself. Then I think about all the lies that men and women have told me from their own stories, lies that pollute and pillage, wound and maim. It is then I realize that what Jesus was saying is the sober truth: there is a liar who is out to murder us. The fact that we find this so hard to believe is in fact a part of the lying. Like Scar, the Great Dragon spins his web of lies and then carefully covers his tracks. Remember, staying covert is part of his strategy.

DEFEATING THE GREAT DRAGON

To keep at the descent, we have to take on the Great Dragon, but this battle will not be won with sword or spear. He won't be brought down by persuasion or argument either. There is only one weapon that will work. It's the only weapon we have, but it will bring him down. It's the truth. We have to know the truth, feel the truth, and then stand on it. Paul gave us this fighting strategy: "Put on the full armor of God so that you can take your stand against the devil's schemes" (Eph. 6:11 NIV). But make no mistake: standing on truth here will not be pretty. This is not standing in agreement or standing in honor. This is a stand of total defiance against the devil's vicious lies. It will feel at times like standing out in the open when hurricane-force winds are ripping past you.

As I was writing this chapter, one of my former students called me to say that he felt he was under spiritual assault. All the academic pressures of being a senior at college, along with the unknowns of his future after graduation, were now being compounded by a lying voice that came to him at night, poisoning his heart. One of the most persistent of the lies he was hearing was that God didn't really love him. He knew it wasn't true, but the force of it felt overwhelming at times. It was a cruel stratagem, one that sought to attack him at a vulnerable moment in his life. I encouraged him to stay in the Father's love, soak himself in the truth, and continue to seek counsel and prayer. Since then, I know he has continued to stand defiantly and persevere in the truth.

But the force of these types of assaults is often intensified by the shame we feel in admitting to others that we are being assaulted. It just sounds too bizarre, too outlandish. Revealing our spiritual struggles will make us look weird. Who talks about that anyway? Isn't this a sign that we are mentally ill, that we are hearing voices in the night? Again, shame is all part of Satan's scheme to keep us divided inside ourselves and alienated from others.

Once I set up a meeting with some dads to think about how to structure a father/son event. The night before the meeting, as I was putting food away after dinner, I suddenly felt this thrust into my mind: *It will never work.* It is hard to describe how those four words immediately deflated me, leaving me debilitated and confused. It felt as if I had been punched in the stomach. It was the enemy jabbing me directly in my old wound, the one that tells me I am a failure, and

---

There is only one weapon that will work. It's the only weapon we have, but it will bring him down. It's the truth.

I was tempted to respond with the same old vow never to fail in front of others. Even after years of fierce resistance, it is still a tender spot. But this time, to keep resisting, I knew what I had to do despite the awkwardness of it. The next morning, after some planning with the dads, I told them in halting words about the assault. Their response was completely unexpected. They gathered around, laid hands on me, and prayed. Not only was shame defeated that day; so was the enemy. We put on the father/son event, and despite the challenges, it worked better than we could have imagined.

But our best inspiration in this fight comes from the work already done by our Commander. We are not battling a dragon with endless reserves of power and strength. We are fighting a vanquished one. Paul reminded us that on the cross Jesus defanged the Great Dragon, subdued him, and then publicly shamed him as a defeated foe (Col. 2:15). This dragon has already been fought and mortally wounded. So at some point in our resistance, he must back off and back away: "Resist the devil, and he will flee from you (James 4:7 NIV).

More inspiration comes when we realize that others are standing with us. This is exactly the point Peter made: "Resist him and be strong in your faith, knowing that your brothers and sisters through-out the world are fellow sufferers with you" (1 Peter 5:9). For years I pictured my stance of resistance as a lonely battle, one in which I found myself struggling to stay upright. But Peter said that we can keep resisting and win the day precisely because we know that others are in the same position, suffering through the same battles. We were never meant to stand alone.

On a recent walk with my friend Carter, he told me of an image that came to him in prayer. We were both on top of separate hills, at our assigned posts, fighting our separate battles to extend the kingdom. What gave him so much inspiration was just seeing me there in active combat from his vantage point. He didn't need to talk to me. He just needed to see me. That's what gave him the strength to keep fighting. When he told me this, I felt surprised at my impact on him and realized something obvious that I had been missing: Carter can't stand on his own either. He needs me and others to stand with him. This is what brings the Great Dragon down, what he can't stand. He must turn and flee.

And now, at the lowest recesses of this descent, in the sweat and grime over battles fought, in the fatigue and strain over distances covered, we discover something unforeseen when we started. The point of learning to fight these dragons wasn't to become a better fighter or a better follower of Jesus. It wasn't even to close the divide between our heads and hearts, although that's what we thought at the beginning. The point was to prepare us for something, to pre-pare us for Someone, to make our hearts ready for the Presence. That's the ascent. That's the next part of the journey.

PRAYER:

Jesus, I know You are the great Warrior. You took on injustice, evil, and the evil one himself. And You conquered with Your resurrection. You are truly the great hero. But I feel so weak and fearful. The thought of the descent, of death, of facing these dragons, leaves me faint. I see the way before me, and yet I falter. I know what I need to do, but I don't know if I have the courage to continue. I need You to meet me in my fear and hesitation, in my pain and confusion. I need You to meet me each day, teaching me to fight, encouraging me to get back up after I fall. I know now that I can't do this alone. I can't do anything without You. But through You, I can do all things. I believe this, but now help me in my unbelief. Close the divide even here, so I can keep at this journey. I love You. Teach me to love You more.

JESUS: *I know your fear. I know your weakness. When I ask you to come and follow Me, I will come and teach you every step of the way. Remember that I am not trying to kill you. I want to make you come alive. This is the way. I showed it by My death and resurrection. Do not fear. Trust Me. I have overcome the world.*

QUESTIONS FOR JOURNALING AND DISCUSSION

1. Pick out a quote or a story from this chapter that stirred something in you. Describe your reaction and why you felt this way.

2. The journey to close the divide always begins with a descent. How does your heart respond to this? With fear, anxiety, readiness, hope, confusion, or something else? What do you think is behind that?

3. How have you already faced the dragon of idolatry? What idols are you still hooked to? What do you need God to do for you now?

4. How have you faced the dragon of shame? Or have you? Has this book helped you face this dragon? If so, how?

5. The evil one is the Great Dragon himself. How do you see the evil one operating in your life to keep you divided? How have you tried to stand against his lies?

6. Read again James 4:7 and 1 Peter 5:9. What encourages you about these verses right now in your own battles with the evil one?

THE ASCENT

What can be seen on earth indicates neither the total absence, nor the manifest presence of divinity, but the presence of a hidden God. Everything bears this stamp.

—**Pascal**[1]

I have always wanted to go up, and it doesn't matter where or how. My favorite part of any plane ride is the acceleration down the runway, the feel of being forced back in my seat, and the quick upturn in elevation as the wheels leave the ground. Skyscrapers also grab my attention. I love to take the elevator up for the commanding view, whether it's the Willis Tower in Chicago or the office buildings downtown. And then there are mountains. One summer, I helped lead a fly-fishing trip to Colorado with a group of fathers and sons. It seemed that everyone was focused on catching the next trout, but I just kept looking up. The peaks kept whispering my name. I wanted to climb.

The first time I did manage to climb mountains in Colorado involved two separate ascents on adjacent peaks, each more than fourteen thousand feet high. I was able to reach the first summit without much trouble, despite the fact that my body had never experienced such altitude. But the second peak nearly undid me.

For the last half mile, the incline kept steepening, and the scree kept me constantly scrambling. The effort required to put one foot in front of the other became monumental. At one point, I wondered if I could even make it, but one thing kept me going: the summit. I wanted to finish the climb and catch the view. And finish it I did, more exhausted and spent than I had felt in a long time. But the panorama from the top is seared into my memory: row after row of serried mountain peaks endlessly pockmarking the landscape, cloud shadows gently undulating over the entire scene, and a vast silence that seemed to swallow it all when the wind momentarily stilled. The pain and toil of the ascent were completely forgotten, replaced by the stark wonder of the moment. I know that I'm not alone in my love for ascending peaks. So many others feel the same way, from the experts who spend their lives doing it to the ordinary weekend climbers like me. When asked, "Why do it?" hikers give various responses: the challenge of the climb, the adventure of it all, the teamwork it takes, the quest it poses, but sooner or later, all answers cluster around the same point: it's the top; it's the summit. Something up there draws us.

Of course, it's the spectacular vista that can't be achieved any other way, but there's more. It's the sense of freedom, of feeling like an eagle, if just for a moment, soaring above the normal daily grind, with the wind caressing our faces and ruffling our hair. But there's even more. We don't just want to feel the wind blow on us. We want it to blow through us. We don't just want the elevation lift around us. We want it in us. Somehow beyond words or understanding, it's the secret engraved on our souls, the longing unbidden

We don't just want the elevation lift around us. We want it in us.

in our hearts. We want to be better than what we are, to somehow be higher, lifted up beyond the tragic and the twisted. We all want to ascend. But this is no mountain peak in the distance. It's right here among us. It's the ascent to become undivided and whole, unashamed and holy. The ascent is in ourselves.

DESCENDING BEFORE ASCENDING

The Scriptures speak in glowing terms of this internal ascent. Isaiah proclaimed that "those who trust in the Eternal One will regain their strength. They will soar on wings as eagles" (40:31). David prayed that God would lead him "to the rock that is higher than I" (Ps. 61:2 NIV)—the rock that is God Himself. And Habakkuk exclaimed, "The Eternal Lord is my strength! He has made my feet like the feet of a deer; He allows me to walk on high places" (3:19). But something has been left out of these depictions of the interior ascent. Each was written in a context that was the exact opposite of any type of "ascended" state. These writers' lives were racked by despair and riddled with insecurity. Isaiah had foreseen the impending devastation of Jerusalem, David was being hounded by his enemies, and Habakkuk had realized that Assyria would one day overrun Israel. Each of them faced something menacing and harrowing: a descent first. Only in that context did they speak of an ascent.

This pattern of descent and ascent is played out in circles larger than just a particular situation. It can be played out over an entire life. Abraham had to pack up and leave Ur to inherit the blessing of the promised land. His descent involved leaving everything familiar to enter a life of complete unknowns. He had no idea where he was going, how long he would travel, or what would happen when he arrived. All he had were the Lord's command to go and the promised blessing. Joseph was sold off as a slave by jealous brothers. Later, he languished in prison on unjust charges for months on end. His long descent abruptly ended when he interpreted Pharaoh's dream and found himself ruling all of Egypt, second only to Pharaoh himself. Moses murdered a man and fled for his life, spending years wandering the trackless wastes of the Midian desert as a forgotten sheepherder. He felt that his life was over, but this descent became his preparation for the great work ahead: leading the Israelites out of Egypt. David was relentlessly chased by Saul even after receiving the kingship. He lived as a fugitive, hiding in caves and constantly fearful for his life. It was the descent required of him before he could ascend to the throne as Israel's greatest king. Each of these stories gives us a pattern of how God works with those who want to walk with Him. And of course, they are but faint etchings of the clearest portrait of this pattern, the Son of God Himself. He descended first into human form, and then further into the bowels of degradation and suffering on the cross. Only then could He ascend to the Father's side, possessing a name above every name and wielding a power above every power.

But the pattern plays out further still. It appears to be the outline of so many of the stories we love. The hero goes through trials and tribulations, apparent defeats and startling setbacks, all of which culminate in a climactic turn of events that end with him coming out victorious. The seemingly endless descents allow his ascent to stand out with striking force and beauty. One of the most popular stories of all time, *Les Misérables*, is a classic portrayal of this descent. Jean Valjean, the convict turned hero, is forever hounded by his nemesis, Javert. Through trial and despair, even tempted with the chance to kill Javert, he keeps trying to do the right thing no matter what it costs him. The descent even has a physical presentation. At one point, Valjean takes the wounded Marius down into the serpentine sewers of Paris, trudging through the filth and muck to escape the pursuing Javert. When all seems lost for our protagonist, Javert suddenly commits suicide, unable to cope with Valjean's mercy. The hero has conquered, but only after a heart-wrenching descent.

For Tolkien, this pattern was perhaps the most memorable trait of a true fairy tale. It is the sudden ascent, that sudden turn of events that gives "a fleeting glimpse of Joy, Joy beyond the walls of the world, poignant as grief. It is the mark of a good fairy-story, of the higher or more complete kind, that however wild its events, however fantastic or terrible the adventures, it can give to child or man that hears it, when the 'turn' comes, a catch of the breath, a beat and lifting of the heart, near to (or indeed accompanied by) tears, as keen as that given by any form of literary art, and having a peculiar quality." [2] His own *Lord of the Rings* is a classic in this regard. After all the terrible adventures Frodo endures on his mission to take the ring into Mordor and destroy it, he can't do it in the end. The ring takes him too. When all seems lost, Gollum bites the ring off Frodo's finger and then falls himself with the ring into the molten lava underneath Mount Doom. The evil of Mordor is forever destroyed, and Frodo and Sam, thinking their lives are over, are instead honored before an innumerable host for their courage and perseverance. Sam expresses his astonishment over such a dramatic turn with this poignant question: "Is everything sad going to come untrue?" When I got to this turn in the story, I felt exactly what Tolkien described: a sudden catch of the breath and a lifting of the heart. From an unknown and largely untapped place inside of me, tears welled up, reflecting a light from another world. For just a moment that light gleamed, and I felt a "fleeting glimpse of Joy."

For just a moment that light gleamed, and I felt a "fleeting glimpse of Joy."

THE SLOGS AND THE BREAKTHROUGHS

But it's one thing to read a story; it's another to live in one. It's one thing to read of the great descents and ascents in the Bible, but in our own lives? What does that look like? How do we take that mountain climb ourselves? How do we soar on wings like eagles, using Isaiah's striking imagery? What does it look like in the normal helter-skelter of life to put our heads and hearts together amid laundry and e-mails, with school pressures and work deadlines, among endless errands and needy children? What is the feel for the ascent in the daily and the normal? I got my best answer to this from an unlikely source: cross-country running.

For years, I coached high school young men through the training required to race a 5K at competitive speeds. I was always amazed at where they started the season compared to how they finished it. But the journey to get there was grueling. We would start with base running, logging endless miles during the summer at a slow pace. Then I would add tempo runs, three to five miles in distance at a faster pace. After a couple of weeks, it was time for interval training. Our bread-and-butter workout became 5x1000m intervals, running each one at an intense pace. To make things even more interesting, we would throw in hill repeats. With all of this arduous training, you would think the race times of these young men would constantly improve. But that rarely happened. More commonly, they would see minimal improvements, with an occasional setback during the race season. But at some point, if they kept at it, something dramatic would happen in one race. All of a sudden, they would sprint through the finish line posting a huge drop in time. It was a breakthrough race. The elation of that moment erased all memories of slogging through the painful training.

This is exactly the feel of the ascent in our lives. It's a descent first, sometimes endless slogging, until the breakthrough comes and we start the ascent. It is persevering to close the divide even when there seems to be little change or even momentary setbacks. It is persisting in the path to surface the lies, listen to the truth, and tell our story to others. It is a refusal to turn back even when the way forward feels uncharted and precarious. All of this slogging is setting us up for the breakthrough, when something drops off our hearts that has until now kept them bound, when we catch a glimpse of delight replacing shame, when a vow is broken, when we experience a freedom that we never knew existed. But the breakthroughs are always a mystery. They can't be timed, programmed, or repeated. They are glimpses of joy that always surprise us. And now we finally begin to understand the road ahead. The descent is our work, the journey that we must take. The ascent is God's work, the mystery that we enter.

One of my friends is a man who has descended deeply, slogging his way through endless obstacles to close the gaping split in his life. Raised in a churchgoing family by a father with an iron fist, he was soon repeating the pattern with his own family. He could give correct answers to any theological question, but that didn't stop him from terrorizing his wife and children with angry outbursts, or curtail his growing dependence on pornography. His fear of being discovered left him one day weeping on the roadside in his car, admitting his utter helplessness and need of the Lord. It was time to begin the descent.

As he began the journey, he knew he had to tell his story, to admit his struggles to others. And then there was more slogging as memories of being relentlessly bullied surfaced, as well as stories of his father's physical abuse. Along with that was dealing with his own judgmental heart. Yet through it all, God showed up in mysterious ways, putting his heart and mind slowly back together. One of the profoundest ways this has happened is with his faith. He admits now that he was probably deceived all those years, thinking he was a Christian and yet having no feel for the Father's love or a heart that could offer it. Yet when I talk to him now, his whole demeanor suffuses humility and hope. He no longer just believes in Jesus. He radiates Jesus. The breakthrough has been remarkable.

I, too, have my own tales of slogging and breakthrough. One of the most memorable has to do with something so shameful that I buried it for years: my own lack of feeling like a man. I grew up with no real bond to any older male. I had some boys with whom I played while growing up, but I was very much content by myself, reading or playing the piano. All of that changed in adolescence. Everything inside me ached for someone, anyone, to coach and encourage me. Yet no one appeared to guide me, so whatever budding sense of manhood I felt was summarily crushed again and again. Whether it involved the girl I longed to date, or the sport I longed to play, or the risk I longed to take, I always listened to my fears and did nothing. The result was tragic. I became stuck at thirteen, largely sexless, a neutered man. To compensate, I stuck to what I was good at, my ability to comprehend ideas and teach them. When I became a pastor, the result was a highly conceptual-ized faith, but underneath was a boy frozen in place, for true mascu-linity is not a concept; it's a feel. Manhood is not an idea to grasp, but an experience to be ushered into. Only Heidi knew of this deep

---

The descent is our work, the journey that we must take. The ascent is God's work, the mystery that we enter.

sadness; she had to live with an emotional thirteen-year-old for years.

The descent to pull all of this up took endless slogging. I had to work to surface all the lies and vows, many of which I have already described in this book. Then I had to persevere in listening to the truth that I was a beloved son, that I had a Father who would coach me, defend me, and usher me into manhood. And finally, I had to tell my story to others, admitting all of this and trying to see myself through their eyes. Yet even with all the slogging, it seemed that this deepest of all divides was impervious to change. How was I to feel like a man with no emotional template to turn to? How was I to become what I had never known, what I had never felt? Here is where God has surprised me with sudden ascents. One of the most dramatic happened in a basement.

Heidi and I were visiting an elderly couple who had nurtured Heidi all her life. Although they were not able to have children, they mentored many teenagers, teaching in the high schools, and even bringing some into their home to live. I loved being around them because they were so personable and approachable. One day, the man took me down into his basement, where he had an extensive woodworking shop. There he carefully explained how each of the machines worked, showing me some of his wood creations. Then he took me over to his hunting guns and told me stories of some of his memorable hunts. Something stirred in me as we talked. It was the thirteen-year-old boy that I had already surfaced, now longing to be mentored and loving the feel of having an older man tell me his stories.

When it came time to leave for the evening, he handed me as a parting gift an old woodworking book, hoping I would find it helpful. But he had already given me something priceless. For the first time perhaps, I felt what I can only describe as a smoke, permeating me, as a campfire does with clothing. It was the smoke of masculinity, staining me with its odor and feel. Only on the trip back did I realize what had happened. I had been marked as a man.

THE BREAKTHROUGH INTO THE PRESENCE

But sooner or later, on this journey toward wholeness, amid the slogs and the breakthroughs, we come to a stark realization. When we started out, we thought the journey would be about mending the great split in our souls, the divide between our heads and hearts. All the labor and effort to close the divide, to become focused and whole, was before us, and we sought to tackle it. It was all about fixing something, healing something, changing something, achieving something. But now we come to understand in the experience of the ascent that we are colliding headlong with something beyond our control. In fact, this journey is not really about doing something at all. It's about receiving someone.

Perhaps the most definitive mapping of the ascent was charted out for us by the apostle Paul as he prayed for the Ephesian church. You would think that Paul would focus his prayers around God's people living exemplary lives and doing great things for His kingdom, or perhaps overcoming trials and working through personal struggles. But Paul didn't go there at all. He prayed that they would have the power to receive someone: "I pray that out of his glorious riches he may strengthen you with power . . . so that Christ may dwell in your hearts through faith" (Eph. 3:16-17 NIV). Apparently, our state is so darkened that we are not able to contain the presence of the One who is the Light of the World. It would be like shining floodlights into the eyes of those who have been living in caves, blinding them instead of helping them. Or it would be like offering a starving man vast quantities of food, sickening him and perhaps killing him. In like manner, we are so used to living in our shame and guilt that the idea of the living, resurrected Jesus coming that close to us doesn't engender hope, but anxiety. One friend recently told me that the idea of Jesus coming to dwell with him made him uncomfortable. There were so many things wrong in his life, so much that he felt ashamed of. In his mind's eye, he pictured himself not being able to turn and face Jesus as He approached. Instead, he turned away, with one arm raised, as if to fend off His presence. What he needed most is what he struggled to receive.

Yet Paul went on to an even higher elevation on this ascent. He prayed for more power, more strength, so that together with other believers, we could "grasp how wide and long and high and deep is the love of Christ" (v. 18 NIV). Again, our need for strength is not so we can accomplish anything. It's about receiving something—this time, a revelation of how cherished and beloved we are, a revelation we can receive only with others who are climbing with us. Paul seems to have implied that if the full weight of Christ's love would fall on us, it would crush us. We couldn't handle it. Our weakened frames need to be strengthened so we can hold such a burden, if we can even speak of love as a burden. But so it seems. And with that strengthening, we can now "know this love that surpasses knowledge" (v. 19 NIV), a love that helps us enter behind the veil of knowing and into the presence of being known and enjoyed. And the final destination: "that you may be filled to the measure of all of the fullness of God." This is why we climb—to break through into the fullness of God. That's the peak. That's the summit.

HEAD VERSUS HEART

And now we approach still another realization as we ascend. Perhaps we had pictured the head and the heart as coming together so that they now collaborate in some kind of fifty-fifty partnership. But the ascent has taken us on another path. It is the experience of being loved, of being fully known and utterly treasured, that unleashes God's fullness inside of us. As one who has had the privilege of higher education and the opportunity to read the great minds, I know the helpfulness of understanding the various systems of thought as well as grappling with the unique ideas of Christianity. These have no small importance in both loving God with our minds and growing in the faith. But the mind was never the summit. To stop here is not only to misunderstand the goal of redemption but also to make the mind a subtle place of idolatry.

The mind was always meant to be a gateway, a portal through which we could discern and receive the truth. But the destination is different. It's the heart. Theology is needed to help us define the borders of the mystery of the faith, but it can never fully enunciate the mystery itself. It is needed to fend off heresy, which only hurts the heart in the end, but the mind can't be the receptacle of the Father's love, something we can only know with the heart. Over and over again, the Bible leads us to see the heart as the central core of our existence, out of which we think and act, the place of connection with the living God. It seems that He never intended to live in our minds; He wants to live in our hearts.

Seeing the mind and heart this way fits into other patterns. For instance, take some of the great minds of the Christian faith and their experiences. Augustine's conversion came after years of intellectual struggle to come to terms with the truth of Christianity. Yet his real conversion had nothing to do with the intellect but with his anguish over his own sexual addictions. Sobbing in a garden one day, he finally yielded his heart as a verse from Romans pierced the darkness of his despair. Thomas Aquinas, the great theologian of the Middle Ages, is known for his massive works filled with razor-sharp thinking. Yet near the end of his life, he experienced a moment of contact with the presence of the living Christ. He could hardly dictate anymore to his secretary, confessing that all he had written seemed like straw to him now. Approaching more present times, Mortimer Adler was a modern philosopher of wide influence. Growing up as an atheist from a nominal Jewish background, he became mesmerized in his twenties with the intellectual acumen of both Augustine and Aquinas. He spent the next fifty years of his life reading and defending the truth of the Christian faith, yet his real conversion was still to come. After walking through a protracted sickness and mild depression, he began weeping as the local church rector prayed over him in the hospital one day. He then started saying the only prayer he knew by heart, the Lord's Prayer, over and over again, meaning every word of it. One night, he suddenly realized that he had taken that final step of faith, opening his heart to the Father, without even realizing it at the time.[3]

More remarkable corroboration concerning the priority of the heart comes from new research on the brain. We now realize that emotion is not a just subset of the brain's functions, but the whole force around which the brain organizes itself.[4] It seems that our rational thinking, although critical, is a subset. The heart is front and center. Pascal, another great intellect of the faith, summarized it elegantly in these words: "The heart has its reasons of which reason knows nothing."[5] Reason can help us climb at points, but it can't take us to the summit. Only through the heart do we close the divide

---

**Reason can help us climb at points,
but it can't take us to the summit.
Only through the heart do we close the
divide between the head and heart.**

between the head and heart. Only there will we experience His presence.

GLIMPSES OF THE PRESENCE

God's presence is one of the overarching themes of the Bible and the most significant for our own hearts because the greatest of the divides is not between our heads and hearts. Neither is it between our outer mask and inner self. It's between ourselves and God. It's the gap that creates the other gaps, the divide that causes the other divides. We have lost that connection, and know instinctively, without being informed, that we have lost it, even if we can't put words to what exactly *it* is. We all sense life as a lock with a missing key, a puzzle with an unknown code. And that unknown code, that missing key, is the presence of God.

When our first parents were banished from the garden, it wasn't just from a place; it was from Someone. They could no longer meet the Lord and walk in the garden with Him in the cool of the day (see Genesis 3:8 NIV). That sense of exile now hangs over everything we do and feel, no matter how much we deny it, suppress it, or ignore it. But one day, the Bible says, the exile will be over, the banishment ended: "See, the home of God is with *His* people. He will live among them; they will be His people, and God Himself will be with them" (Rev. 21:3). Between the present exile and the future restoration, we find the rest of the story of the Bible, a circuitous tale of man's rebellion and forgetfulness. But amid all the tragic lapses, there are tantalizing glimpses of Joy, glimpses of the Presence.

In the Old Testament arrangement, God's presence tended to be something more exterior, whether the pillar of cloud that led the Israelites through the desert or the Holy of Holies that lay behind the veil in the temple. As such, the Presence was both longed for and guarded, desired and feared. One of the saddest moments in the biblical narrative is when the prophet Ezekiel saw the Presence departing from the temple. God was no longer to be found in that part of the temple called the Holy of Holies because no one was seeking Him; instead, everyone had turned to his own way, replaying once more the original fall. But the promise was given at that same time of something new, something momentous: "I will give them *a new will*—an undivided heart—and plant a new spirit within them; I will remove their *cold*, stony heart and replace it with a *warm* heart of flesh" (Ezek. 11:19).

That momentous event happened when Jesus appeared. He came not just to forgive our sins and clean up our lives but to start a new order of things, where our hearts are no longer divided, where the presence of God is no longer just exterior. In that watershed moment on the cross, the veil between the Holy of Holies and the rest of the temple was ripped from top to bottom, not only so believers could have unimpeded access to God but also that God's presence could go out into believers. The Holy of Holies is no longer a place to go; it's here, inside. Our hearts now become the new Holy of Holies.

What could this mean? Start by recalling those exalted moments in your life, when you felt you had brushed up against God's presence. Maybe you were walking inside a cathedral, where the vaulted ceilings and upward projections mixed with that immense space, and you felt your own soul being pulled up with the architecture into something mysterious and transcendent. Perhaps it was that moment when you walked on the beach at sunset, and the fading light tinged the clouds a rosy-purplish glow, only to dim quickly into grayness. You were mesmerized, drawn into this fleeting portal of beauty, drawn to something calling behind the beauty. Maybe it happened while listening to a full symphony or a solo artist, when the music tapped and awoke some ancient, unvoiced longing for something more, something forgotten. One of these exalted moments happened to me in the least likely of places, my Ford pickup.

When my family saw the first Narnia movie, we loved the music so much that I bought the sound track soon after. On the way to a meeting one evening in my truck, I opened the CD and began to listen to it for the first time. As I neared my destination, the track that accompanies Lucy's first entrance into Narnia through the wardrobe door began to play. Precisely at that instant, I, too, felt a door open into another world, with its air swiftly rushing out, blowing through me with all of its piercing freshness and stabbing delight. Suddenly, I was sobbing uncontrollably. I parked the truck and slowly regained my composure. Replaying the music, I hoped perhaps for the door to open again. But this time it was just the beautiful music of flutes and strings. Apparently, there is only one knob to this door, and it's not on our side. The door opens and shuts without our permission or control. These are our holy moments, when we are suddenly ushered into the transcendent, into the Presence. They sear us with longing for something lost, something from which we have been exiled, and we awaken back into the normal, aching for more.

Jesus came to take these moments and make them something more than just fleeting glimpses. He wants to bring them much closer into our lives of exile. He wants to do what is impossible by

---

The Holy of Holies is no longer a place to go; it's here, inside. Our hearts now become the new Holy of Holies.

human effort: plant that glimpse of joy—His joy—into the barren and fractured wasteland of the heart: "I have told you these things so that my joy may be in you and that your joy may be complete" (John 15:11 NIV). What we are exiled from cannot really be found in cathedrals or sunsets or enchanting music. It can only be found in the Presence. And that Presence wants to take up residence inside us: "Anyone who loves Me will listen to My voice and obey," Jesus said. "The Father will love him, and We will draw close to him and make a dwelling place within him" (John 14:23). This is the stunning surprise of the ascent.

STORIES OF ASCENT

Offering anything prescriptive or formulaic at this point feels improper, even jarring. It doesn't fit because the way Jesus comes to make His home inside of us is as unique as our stories, as different as our fingerprints. Take, for instance, this story from a dear friend of Heidi's, an artist whose beautiful paintings echo the growing beauty in her heart. Growing up with a bipolar father, she experienced his chaotic life as a stream of mixed messages that could never be trusted. Into this vacuum of instability came the lie that she was on her own. It manifested in thoughts like these that constantly played out in her mind: *I have to figure this out . . . God would want me to take care of this . . . I can't rest until this is resolved . . . I have to make sure everyone understands where I am coming from.* To further protect herself, she felt that she had to be powerful and stay in control. She later gave this persona a name: "powerful child." When circumstances didn't go her way, when financial ruin entered her life, when a child was born with medical issues, she became angry. She no longer felt powerful. She couldn't control it or figure it out on her own.

The breaking point came when her marriage dissolved. With that loss came the loss of her home and all steady income. She found herself over fifty and having to look for work. Along with all of the grief and stress, she developed shingles accompanied by painful boils. The long descent ended in a moment of crisis when she found herself lying on the floor of her newly rented house, crying, out of control, completely powerless. It was there that the Presence showed up: "I felt God's presence like a blanket on me. I was able to imagine myself swinging in a porch swing with my Father, with my head on His lap, neither of us speaking, but my core was able to experience peace. In the following days, during those terrifying moments in court, or at night, or in my car, I would go back to the porch swing image. I could feel my Father's breath on my neck like He was holding me and rocking me." She was still powerless, but now she felt the Power, the true Father she had always longed for. Her situation didn't change, but everything inside started to. She felt cared for, loved, protected. But this onetime glimpse is now something she is learning to practice every day. She has learned to turn off the radio and the TV and to sit in silence before Him, journaling and praying. This is how she enters the presence of the Father who still holds her on that porch swing. Her final comment is so telling: "It's all God's doing. Even my willingness comes from Him."

For the sake of contrast, take another story from another era, this time from Blaise Pascal, a Frenchman living in the 1600s. Pascal was a mathematical prodigy as well as a scientific pioneer, but through the influence of his younger sister, he began to seek after truth and the living God. He went on to author one of the most incisive defenses of the Christian faith ever written, the *Pensées*. But the convincing factor for him personally wasn't all the converging lines of evidence that he described in the book. It was the ascent he experienced. After his death, a piece of parchment was found folded up and sewn into his coat. On it was written the experience of the Presence that marked him for the rest of his life. It opens this way: "Fire. God of Abraham, God of Isaac, God of Jacob, not of philosophers and scholars. Certainty, certainty, heartfelt, joy, peace. God of Jesus Christ." It continues by quoting Scripture, along with his responses. At one point he simply wrote this: "Joy, joy, joy, tears of joy." And near the end of the parchment, we find these words: "Sweet and total renunciation. Total submission to Jesus Christ."[6] It was this moment that changed everything. It was the Presence. God was no longer a concept but a felt reality. Pascal would spend the last eight years of his life in that sweet renunciation and total submission to Jesus Christ, struggling to live in it and write out of it. It was that glimpse of joy that kept him moving toward God, despite family tragedy and chronic sickness, until his death.

STAYING IN THE PRESENCE

But ascending into the Presence is not meant to be just a rapturous experience. It's a daily discipline. The hardest thing for most of us is the most needful thing: to be still before God. There we must learn to wait without demanding or dictating terms. For those who want a suntan, there is one absolute necessity—get out in the sun. After that, nothing can be forced. It's the very presence of the sun that will do the rest. Likewise, we can't force God to show up. But what we can do is shut out the world's incessant babbling and be still and silent, listening attentively to our hearts and to His Word. For me, the best part of each day has become the early-morning moments with my cup of coffee, my Bible, and my journal. It is a structured time of silence, where I give myself over to being with the Presence. It is my attempt to get out in the sun. But the call to stay in the

Presence will take us to a deeper listening, this time to the voice behind His Word, to the voice of God Himself.

For me, the whole idea of God's voice was something I longed for and yet dismissed, something I hoped for and yet doubted. Looking back on it all now, I realize that my conflicted views were indicative of the core issues of my heart. The fact that my prayer life was a monologue suggested that the thick walls I had erected around myself, keeping everyone out including God, had left me in a vast interior wasteland of aloneness. The fact that so much of my experience of the Bible stayed in the conceptual suggested the terrible chasm between my head and heart. Reading the Bible was just another part of that same pattern, concepts and ideas that I couldn't move past my intellect. For years I wondered, *Where is my heart? Who or what has stolen it?* But when I began to understand the divide, I realized the culprit. It was *me*. I had used my own intellect to beat my heart into submission, locking it away in a dark and musty closet, somewhat akin to what a cruel parent does to a child. As I tackled the divide and opened the closet, I began to hear my heart for the first time. But in so doing, something unexpected came. I began to hear another voice, God's voice. Prayer shifted from monologue to dialogue. The Scriptures shifted from intellectual musings to heart encounters.

I know that the whole issue of God's voice is fraught with peril on a number of levels, theological and emotional. It can be used to give a peremptory authority to someone's teaching or decision. It can be used by those with some form of psychosis, whose own break from reality includes the voices in their heads. It can be used by those so paralyzed with fear, so unformed in their own sense of self, that they cannot make decisions unless they hear a voice. Yet what may be perilous is not necessarily false. What may be easily distorted is not necessarily unprofitable. If the God of the

Bible spoke the worlds into existence and continually spoke to individuals all throughout the Bible, it seems likely that the pattern of His speaking would continue on. Perhaps He even wants us to hear Him. But how do you know if it's His voice?

Often I will ask others, "How do you know the voice of your mother or father?" The answer is not readily apparent, for there's nothing you can point to. But that's the whole point. Unless you've never known your parents, you've simply been with them for so long that you just know their voices. That's exactly how we learn the voice of God. It's time spent with Him. There is a tone, a texture, a timbre to that voice that we learn to recognize along the way. Yet in the beginning, even Samuel the prophet had to be told, by Eli, that it was the Lord's voice he was hearing (1 Sam. 3). As we start this journey, we, too, will need mentors to guide us and help us sort out any confusion we have here.

In my own journey of listening, the words of the Bible become individualized for me. It doesn't change the meaning of Scripture, but it comes now from a person who knows my story and sadness, who understands my flaws and longings, who is more aware of me than I could ever be, yet loves me beyond words. In that voice, I feel known. I feel heard and felt. It is the Presence that has changed so many things in me.

Often His words to me are simple encouragements, perhaps because that was so lacking in my formative years. He continually encourages me with simple directives, ones repeated throughout

---

In the encouragements, reminders, and questions, I feel the Father personally coaching me. It's what any good father wants to do for his son or daughter.

the Bible: *Trust Me. I am with you. You don't need to be afraid.* Just recently, I was thinking through Jeremiah 31:3: "I have loved you with an everlasting love—out of faithfulness I have drawn you *close.*" As I thought about my lifelong struggle to allow others to love me, I simply heard the Lord urging me: *"Let Me love you."* At other times, it moves beyond encouragement. He gently pushes or reminds me: *"I am here, but you can't control Me. Look to Me, not to your problems."* Again, these reminders are given by One who knows my heart, my story, and my core sins. Then on rare occasions, He will question me, deeply probing my heart, gently but firmly. Once when I was struggling with whether to plan a backpacking trip with some fathers and sons, I heard this while driving: *"Why do you always have to be doing something in ministry? Why can't you just go and enjoy Me? Do you have any idea how much I love you?"* The rapid-fire questions stunned me then and still cause me to ponder today. In the encouragements, reminders, and questions, I feel the Father personally coaching me. It's what any good father wants to do for his son or daughter. It's what the Father wants to do for all of us.

But a few words of caution: We never get all the guidance we feel we need. Nor do we get all the answers to our questions. We get what He knows we need, not what we think we need. There will still be troubling theological issues, times of wandering, and even inscrutable suffering. We must open ourselves totally to the Father and be willing to obey whatever comes, for we are dealing with Someone whose love for us is unrelenting. At times He will ask us to do things that seem unreasonable or even impossible in order to make us more like His Son. And He will use whatever He needs to—including irritation, trial, and tragedy—to bring us to the point where we can more fully receive His love and presence. Remember, that's the ascent. That's where all of this is heading.

THE FINAL ASCENT

But a final ascent awaits, a complete closing of the divide, when faith becomes sight, love becomes fullness, and fleeting glimpse becomes unending gaze. What that final ascent will be like, we have only intriguing clues from the Bible; tales from those who have started, only to return; and the unmet longings of our hearts, still hoping, still waiting. Yet it is enough. We are now asked to "fix our eyes not on what is seen, but on what is unseen" (2 Cor. 4:18 NIV).

I got my own front row seat to this final ascent as our family walked my mother through her last days of terminal cancer. I have already mentioned what happened as I learned her story. But there was more to learn during those final days. Her words and images were precious to all of us as we saw the chasm between this world and the next become tissue-paper thin, for this final ascent is about closing that last divide. Once she made this comment: "It won't be long now; He's holding my hand." And on another occasion, these poignant words came out: "There is joy on both sides: joy in staying here or joy in going."

Another time, when her lips were moving, my sister asked what she was saying. Her reply? "I'm talking to angels." My sister said, "Oh, are they singing?" Mom answered, "Yes."

And of course, there were funny moments too. Feeling the impending loss, my sister expressed her grief this way: "Mom, I'm going to miss you so much." Mom didn't skip a beat: "Oh? Where are you going?"

Three days before her death, when she could hardly lift her head, her indomitable servant's heart was still apparent: "Has everybody eaten breakfast?" But her last recorded words were simply these: "Lord, help me."

I believe Mom made the final ascent so well, with such peace and with so little fear, precisely because she had spent her life dying and descending, finding real life in Christ. When actual death finally came, she was just doing what she had always done, dying to live, descending to ascend. Her story is not just a commentary on the ascent but a legacy she leaves to all of us. We, too, can fix our eyes on what is unseen, on what is coming. Perhaps George MacDonald said it best at the end of his *Phantastes*, "Yet I know that good is coming to me—that good is always coming; though few have at all times the simplicity and the courage to believe it." [7]

Yes, that good is coming.

May we have the simplicity and courage to believe it.

PRAYER:

Jesus, I understand. My ache to ascend, to find the life I have longed for, connects to Your ache to come and live in us, to live in me. Yet I am so weak and needy. I don't even know how to receive the weight of Your presence. I don't even know how to take in the fullness of Your love. I need others to help me. I need You to show me. I am willing to slog, but I need You to break through my dullness of mind and my confusion. It is the miracle of Your presence that will change everything in me, and one day will change everything else around me. Come and do more than I could ever ask or imagine. Take me deeper into Your presence. I want You now more than anything.

JESUS: *What you have asked for is what I long to give. Do not despair at the time it takes. I am preparing you to become a worthy vessel for My presence. Let Me be your Good Shepherd. Learn My voice and follow My leading. I will take you into green pastures and lead you beside clear waters. I love you, and I will never leave you.*

QUESTIONS FOR JOURNALING AND DISCUSSION

1. Pick out a quote or a story from this chapter that aroused something in you. Describe your reaction and why you felt that way.

2. Les Misérables is a classic story of the hero's descent before his triumphant ascent. What are some of your favorite stories or movies that show the same pattern?

3. Describe an experience that you've had of God's presence, a moment of glimpsing that joy.

4. Read through Ephesians 3:16–21, Paul's mapping of the ascent. What about this prayer intrigues you? Confuses you? Encourages you? Put words to what you need God to do with your heart right now.

5. How do you see your own head and heart coming together? What do you need to slog through right now? Where do you need God to give you a breakthrough?

6. What has been your experience of listening to God? Do you feel His personal coaching and presence? What questions do you have about this?

CONCLUSION
STUMBLING IN THE DAY

*Often a deep and fervent look at Christ is the
best prayer: I look at Him and He looks at me.*

—Mother Teresa [1]

Yesterday, I could feel it coming on me—again. It was a slow osmosis from one corner of my mind, until my whole brain felt overrun with it: anxiety. Then came the inevitable effects. I become inwardly focused, almost narcissistic, to try to stop myself from going out of control. My friend Daniel came over to the house with a friend to practice music for his upcoming wedding. Instead of being engaged and excited for him, I felt myself withdrawing, faking as much connection as I could muster. What caused the anxiety to begin this time? My triggers can come from several different arenas, a big deadline to meet, a large audience to teach, a risky subject to broach; but this one was about money. Since the start of writing this book some eight months ago, the ministry I lead has gotten by in terms of finances. But the summer drought was coming. I could see the pool of finances drying up. The whole situation felt like a sickening repeat of what I described in the introduction.

I tried to take an afternoon nap to get my mind off of it. No luck. I tried to speak truth to myself, using Scriptures about trust and about the Lord's provision. Still no help. I shared my struggle with Heidi at the kitchen table. She listened and tried to encourage me, but I felt no better. I tried to listen to the Father and His personal encouragements to me. Yet even here, I could find no relief. The onslaught reached a tipping point, where the anxiety, now mixed with fear, went on a rampage through me. I wanted to do anything to get rid of it. I could feel myself writing another resignation speech to the ministry board. Then I realized that I would have to change some of the material in the book. To leave it the way it was would be to exaggerate the truth of some of the stories. Perhaps what I had written was misleading, even wrong. My mind reeled with all that I would have to take back. The thought crossed my mind of quitting everything and going to work in a coffee shop, where life would at least be predictable and known. The old foe of anxiety had seemingly conquered me and then completely sundered me—again. What I knew and what I felt now occupied two entirely different universes.

I tell you all of this so you will have no illusions about me or about the path charted out in this book. Even after all the work I have done in my life, even after teaching and mentoring others in this journey, even after writing this book, I still find myself in desperate places at times, confused, wondering, doubting. I was slogging to stay in God's presence, slogging and sinking.

But something totally unexpected happened. In the midst of the worst of the anxiety, I opened my laptop to look at my e-mails, trying to do something productive. One caught my eye from a local church. As I read it, I was stunned. It said that they were excited to begin supporting the ministry financially on a regular basis, with significant funding. In a matter of seconds, I could feel the anxiety dissipate, yielding to amazement, and then joy. It was the breakthrough; Jesus had broken through. I could feel His presence—again.

I took a walk outside to thank Jesus for His deliverance, His provision, and His rescue of me. I became aware of His awareness of me. Again. I looked at Him, realizing that He was looking at me. I could feel the deep strength pouring back into me, reminding me that I could keep going now, that nothing mattered except His presence, that I could receive His love for me as a man and a fellow brother, that I could return His love by loving Him with all of my heart and then love others out of that fullness. I had stumbled but not fallen. The Presence came. Jesus came. And He changed everything—again.

Let us seek His presence with all our hearts and struggle to live there, whatever it takes, whatever it costs, wherever it leads. It is the healing of our divided souls. It is the *only* healing for our divided souls.

One day it will be the healing of the entire world.

Come, Lord Jesus, come.

APPENDIX
GUIDED SILENT TIMES

Here are a few examples of guided silent times that I have used with individuals and groups. They are a way to help you get into God's presence and soak in His truth. This is how we begin to close the divide between our heads and hearts and let His presence heal and transform us. Although I give only four, the basic format holds true for any Scripture: preparing your heart, digging into Scripture, and then listening. Plan to spend thirty minutes. Entering His presence can't be rushed. Bring your Bible and journal and find a quiet, safe place with no distractions.

Being silent with God is a difficult task for many, at least at first. Getting your mind quiet is the first hurdle. Being attentive to Him is the second hurdle. And then listening is often a third hurdle. You may find yourself being frustrated or confused at times. This is all part of the process. Ask God to teach you how to be quiet and to hear His voice. Trust me: He wants to do that.

God's voice comes primarily through the Scriptures. Ecclesia Bible Society's recent translation of the Bible, published by Thomas Nelson, is in fact titled *The Voice*. But God also wants to come into our lives and personally coach us by His Holy Spirit. It is part of our heritage as believers and part of learning to live in His presence.

Don't try to overanalyze or screen what you sense from the Lord. Just write it down as you think you understand it, words as well as images. Most of us also need help in discerning God's voice. It is important to have a trusted spiritual mentor that you can go to for questions and validation.

It is also important to note that these guided silent times are not a formula. Our job is to be quiet and attentive, and to get into His presence. How God comes to us and reveals Himself to us is always His mysterious work. Finally, be willing to obey and walk in the truth of whatever comes. That's how we stay in His presence and grow deeper in the joy He wants to give us.

With all that said, the experience of being silent with Him will teach you in ways that I cannot possibly tell you beforehand. Let Him surprise you. It's all part of the ascent!

SILENT TIME #1

Preparation: Read John 15:9–12. Jesus invites us to remain in His love for us. We are invited into this each and every day. To attempt to stay there forces us to recognize all the other places where our hearts remain distracted, our idols and our sins. Take a few moments and be quiet, confessing all the places where your heart has been recently. Tell Jesus that you want to accept His invitation right now.

Scripture: Read John 15:1–12. Pick a verse or two that pops out at you. Write it out and then journal your thoughts about it.

Listening:

- Is there anything that Jesus wants to tell you about what you just wrote? Ask Him. Stay still and record any ideas or images that come.

- In verse 9, Jesus says that the love He felt with His Father is the love He has for us. Take some time to be still and consider how Jesus feels about you. How does He feel about your presence with Him now? Ask Him. Be silent as you think about His delight in you. Finish by recording what this was like for you.

SILENT TIME #2

Preparation: Read Psalm 32:1–5. Give the Father any sins or worries that are blocking you from being with Him—simply do what verse 5 says. Then rest in the blessing that is promised in verse 1.

Scripture: Read the rest of Psalm 32, verses 6–11. Select a verse that strikes you. Write it out, along with your thoughts about it.

Listening:

- Try to envision God as a hiding place for you, as mentioned in verse 7. What do you see? What songs do you think He is singing over you?

- The Lord promises to guide you and watch over you in verse 8. Where do you need that guidance and care right now? Is there any personal guidance or affirmation that He wants to give you? Be silent and listen.

- Finally, picture His unfailing love surrounding you as in verse 10, and rest in that a few moments. Record thoughts, images, or words that come to you during this time of listening.

SILENT TIME #3

Preparation: Read John 10:11. Spend a few moments thanking Jesus for being such a good Shepherd. Confess any places where you have refused His shepherding or strayed away.

Scripture: Read John 10:1–11. Pick out a verse or two that seems important. Write it down and journal your thoughts and feelings.

Listening: Read John 10:27. Ask for ears to hear Jesus' voice. Then ask Him if there is anything He wants to say to you about the verses you wrote in your journal. Record anything that comes to you.

SILENT TIME #4

Preparation: Read I Peter 5:7. Then cast all your anxiety, worries, burdens, and sins on Jesus. Open your heart and ask for His forgiveness and peace.

Scripture: Read Paul's prayer for the church in Ephesians 3:16–19. Paul prayed for two things: (1) for the strength to have Christ dwell in us; and (2) for the power to experience His love with others. Write out the entire prayer, marking words or phrases that strike you. Then journal about what you marked, your thoughts, feelings, questions. Also journal about anything you know is blocking you from Jesus' love and presence.

Listening:

- Pray Paul's prayer back to the Father for yourself and for loved ones.

- Ask Jesus, "Is there anything I don't understand that is blocking me from experiencing more of Your presence and love?" Record any thoughts and/or images.

- Read Ephesians 3:20 and thank Jesus for all that He is going to do.

NOTES

INTRODUCTION

1. Thomas à Kempis, *Of the Imitation of Christ* (London: Suttaby & Co., 1883), 147.

PART I

1. Augustine, *City of God*, tr. Gerald G. Walsh et al. (New York: Doubleday, 1958), 309.
2. J. R. R. Tolkien, *The Letters of J. R. R. Tolkien*, ed. Humphrey Carpenter (Boston: Houghton Mifflin, 1981), 110.

CHAPTER I

1. Alexandre Dumas, *The Count of Monte Cristo* (New York: Random House, 1996), 174.
2. *Indiana Jones and the Last Crusade*, directed by Steven Spielberg (Hollywood: Paramount Pictures, 1989).
3. Dean Potter, PrAna, Dean Potter: Focus // Inside Game Episode 3, YouTube, 2 min. 49 sec., 4/9/12, https://www.youtube.com/watch?v=kGil-4INgdc.
4. Ibid.
5. Ibid.

CHAPTER 2

1. Fyodor Dostoyevsky, "Notes from the Underground" in *Great Short Works of Fyodor Dostoevsky,* trans. David Magarshack (New York: Harper & Row, 1968), 376.
2. *Walk the Line*, directed by James Mangold (2005; Los Angeles: Twentieth Century Fox, 2006), DVD.

CHAPTER 3

1. Dietrich Bonhoeffer, *The Cost of Discipleship*, trans. R. H. Fuller and Irmgard Booth (New York: Touchstone, 1995), 89.
2. See John H. Sailhamer, *The Expositor's Bible Commentary*, ed. Frank E. Gaebelein (Grand Rapids: Zondervan, 1990), 51.

PART II

1. Dante, *The Inferno*, tr. John Ciardi (New York: New American Library, 2003), 23–24.
2. Augustine, *The Confessions*, tr. John K. Ryan (New York: Doubleday, 1960), 180.
3. *A Beautiful Mind*, directed by Ron Howard (Universal City, CA: Universal Studios, 2002), motion picture.

CHAPTER 4

1. Michka Assayas, *Bono: In Conversation with Michka Assayas* (New York: Riverhead, 2005), 53.

CHAPTER 5

1. Matthew Henry, *Commentary on the Whole Bible*, vol. 3, *Job to Song of Solomon*, Christian Classics Ethereal Library, http://www.ccel.org/ccel/henry/mhc3.Ps.lix.html, commentary on Psalm 58, accessed June 23, 2014.
2. Derrick Coleman, NFL Network, Derrick Coleman (Seattle Seahawks): The Sound of Silence in the NFL, YouTube, 4 min. 18 sec., 1/12/14, https://www.youtube.com/watch?v=HW51d5Om614.

CHAPTER 6

1. Augustine, *The Confessions*, 277.
2. Curt Thompson, *Anatomy of the Soul* (Carol Stream, IL: Tyndale, 2010), 109–10.
3. Ibid. xiv.
4. *The King's Speech*, directed by Tom Hooper (UK Film Council/See-Saw Films/Bedlam Productions, 2010), motion picture.

PART III

1. *The Matrix*, directed by the Wachowski Brothers, Burbank, CA: Warner Bros. Pictures/Sydney, AU, Roadshow Entertainment, 1999, film.
2. J. R. R. Tolkien, *The Fellowship of the Ring* (New York: Houghton Mifflin Company, 1994), 260.
3. Leo Tolstoy, *Anna Karenina*, trans. Joel Carmichael (New York: Bantam, 1981), 849–50.
4. C. S. Lewis, *The Last Battle* (New York: Harper Collins, 1998), 196.

CHAPTER 7

1. C. S. Lewis, *Mere Christianity* (New York: Harper Collins, 2001), 227.
2. *The Lion King*, directed by Roger Allers and Rob Minkoff (Burbank, CA: Walt Disney, 1994), film.

CHAPTER 8

1. Pascal, *Pensées*, trans. A. J. Krailsheimer (London: Penguin, 1995), 142.
2. J. R. R. Tolkien, *On Fairy Tales*, http://brainstorm-services.com/wcu-2004/fairystories-tolkien.pdf, pp. 22–23, accessed June 2, 2014.
3. Kelly James Clark, ed., *Philosophers Who Believe* (Downers Grove, IL: InterVarsity Press, 1993), 215–16.
4. Curt Thompson, *Anatomy of the Soul*, 90.
5. Pascal, *Pensées*, 127.
6. Ibid., 285–86.
7. George MacDonald, *Phantastes: A Faërie Romance* (London: J. M. Dent & Sons, n.d.), 237.

CONCLUSION

1. Mother Teresa, *No Greater Love* (Novato, CA: New World Library, 1997), 7.

ABOUT THE AUTHOR

Bill Delvaux is a graduate of Duke University and Trinity Evangelical Divinity School. He first served as a youth minister and church planter and then worked as a Bible teacher and running coach at Christ Presbyterian Academy in Nashville, Tennessee. After twenty years of classroom teaching, he felt God's promptings to step out and begin something new, so with a team of committed friends he started Landmark Journey Ministries. The focus of this ministry is to help others connect to their own hearts and to the heart of God. He is also the author of *Landmarks: Turning Points on Your Journey Toward God.*

Bill enjoys reading, biking, and backpacking. His greatest claim to fame is being married to his wife Heidi for twenty-eight years. His other claim is having two grown daughters, Abigail and Rachel. He and his family currently reside in Franklin, Tennessee.

For more information about Landmark Journey Ministries or to get Bill's weekly blog, please visit the website at landmarkjourney ministries.com. You can also follow his daily posts at facebook.com /LandmarkJourneyMinistries or at twitter.com/BillDelvaux. To contact Bill with questions or to request a speaking engagement, please email him at landmarkjourney@gmail.com.

REFRACTION

GOD ALIGNS PEOPLE OF FAITH TO HIS PURPOSES

Thomas Nelson's Refraction collection of books offers biblical responses to the biggest issues of our time, topics that have been tabooed or ignored in the past. The books will give readers insights into these issues and what God says about them, and how to respond to others whose beliefs differ from ours in a transparent and respectful way. Refraction books cross theological boundaries in an open and honest way, through succinct and candid writing for a contemporary, millenial-minded reader.

LEARN MORE AT REFRACTIONBOOKS.COM

| NOW AVAILABLE | NOW AVAILABLE | NOW AVAILABLE | APRIL 2015 | JULY 2015 |